EARTH-SHELTERED
LANDSCAPES

EARTH-SHELTERED LANDSCAPES

*Site Considerations
for Earth-sheltered Environments*

David Douglas DeBord
Thomas R. Dunbar

VNR VAN NOSTRAND REINHOLD COMPANY

New York

Printed in the United States
Designed by Sol Schurman

Published by Van Nostrand Reinhold Company Inc.
135 West 50th Street
New York, New York 10020

Van Nostrand Reinhold Company Limited
Molly Millars Lane
Wokingham, Berkshire RG11 2PY, England

Van Nostrand Reinhold
480 La Trobe Street
Melbourne, Victoria 3000, Australia

Macmillan of Canada
Division of Canada Publishing Corporation
164 Commander Boulevard
Agincourt, Ontario M1S 3C7, Canada

16 15 14 13 12 11 10 9 8 7 6 5 4 3 2 1

Library of Congress Cataloging in Publication Data

DeBord, David Douglas, 1946–
  Earth-sheltered landscapes.

  Bibliography: p.
  Includes index.
  1. Earth sheltered houses. 2. Dwellings—Energy
conservation. 3. Building sites. 4. Landscape architecture. I. Dunbar, Thomas
R., 1947-   . II. Title.
TH4819.E27D43 1985   690′.8   84–20892
ISBN 0-442-21891-5

Contents

Preface

The 1973 oil embargo awakened all of us to a new meaning of the word "energy." Energy suddenly became synonymous with high costs, and those costs kept rising and surpassing levels once thought unreachable. The tripling of oil prices in one year and the corresponding increasing expense of other fuels forced us to reassess both the quantity and the costs of our energy expenditures. The energy crisis was upon us and it was a shock to us all (fig. P-1).

However, the crisis did not suddenly arise in 1973. We had been moving toward it for a long time, and the embargo was simply a dramatic event that made us look at our energy uses differently than in the past. Although we had always been able to drive the largest car we could afford without much concern for its fuel efficiency, suddenly we found that we could not afford to pay for the fuel it consumed. As we adjusted our family budgets to accommodate the increased cost, the fuels that had been so readily available became in such short supply that the country almost returned to the World War II system of fuel rationing.

We had been raised knowing that the physical environment within our shelters could be controlled by simply adjusting the setting on the wall thermostat (fig. P-2). After 1973 we learned, however, that the slightest change in that setting resulted in a substantial change in our fuel bill. The entire relationship between comfort in our shelters and the means of achieving that comfort underwent extensive reevaluation.

Why was housing so dramatically affected by the energy crises of the seventies? The easy answer is the great increase in fuel costs. Before the seventies the interior climate of our homes was controlled to satisfy our personal comfort. This usually meant that inside temperatures were kept between 69 and 72 degrees F. The amount of fuel needed to maintain that range was low in cost and readily available. After the decade, however, it became obvious that it would take more money to buy the same amount of a less readily available fuel.

There is a second answer to explain why our homes were so affected by the events of the seventies. Before the embargoes and leaps in fuel costs, our homes were constructed with little concern for or awareness of their massive energy needs. With cheap fuels, the energy efficiency of our homes was unimportant. It did not matter if we oriented our homes away from the warming winter sun, since we could simply use more inexpensive fuel to stay warm. Likewise, if in the hot summer sun penetrated into the home, the air conditioner worked hard, consuming more fuel, but the cost impact was still slight.

Before the energy crisis we were able to ignore the dramatic influences the environment had on our shelters. Houses were constructed taking our ability to adjust the wall thermostat for granted rather than basing them on climatic criteria. Our lack of understanding of the en-

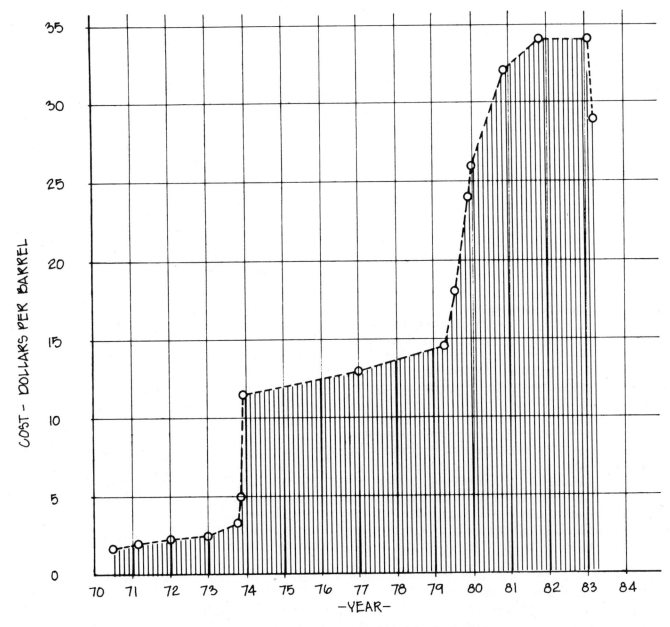

P–1. Oil prices have risen from under three dollars per barrel in 1972 to over thirty dollars in the 1980s.

vironment has led us directly to our current crisis.

The high cost of energy has caused many people to adjust their thinking about how basic shelters should be designed and constructed. A movement toward more and better insulation has been growing. Energy-efficient double- and triple-glazed windows have largely replaced the standard inefficient windows of just a few years ago (table P–1). Efficient water heaters, furnaces, and woodburning stoves have all replaced their inefficient counterparts in the house of yesterday.

Table P-1 Energy Efficiency of Window Areas

Window Type	U-Value *
Single glaze	1.13
Double glaze with $\frac{1}{4}$'' air space	0.65
Double glaze with $\frac{5}{16}$'' air space	0.62
Double glaze with $\frac{1}{2}$'' air space	0.58
Triple glaze with $\frac{1}{4}$'' air space	0.47
Triple glaze with $\frac{1}{2}$'' air space	0.36

* U-Value = The number of Btus (British thermal unit: a unit used to measure quantity of heat) that will pass through a square foot of glazing, per hour, per degree of temperature difference from one side of the glazing to the other.

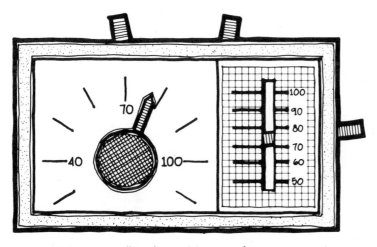

P-2. Wall thermostats allowed a capricious use of energy.

Just as important is the fact that people have begun to realize that the environment does have a great influence on the energy efficiency of a structure. This realization has meant that people are trying to design shelters that are responsive to the environment and able to benefit from its influences rather than design houses that ignore environmental influences and thus become negatively affected by those influences. This change in attitude has resulted in the design and construction of shelters that incorporate active-solar, passive-solar, earth-sheltering, and other energy-efficient environmentally based criteria.

These new designs have required that designers gain a renewed awareness of what the environmental influences are. It has also created new challenges in site design, particularly in those for earth-sheltered structures.

Earth-sheltered landscapes present a particular challenge to site design. Earth-sheltered structures have their own set of site-design requirements that can be quite different from those of other types of structures. Basic good design principles still apply, but the application of those principles requires different emphasis. Proper understanding of the natural elements and of the applicable basic design principles is essential to attain a quality solution to that challenge.

The chapters that follow discuss those natural elements and basic design principles. This book is intended to be used in conjunction with many other references, but the guidelines established here will enable the reader to erect an effective earth-sheltered landscape, whether he or she is a design professional, student, or prospective home builder. A wealth of information is available and the authors hope readers will use these other sources to supplement the guidelines established in *Earth-sheltered Landscapes*.

Earth-sheltered structures are an important part of this country's housing future. Proper construction and design of these structures are critical. With its emphasis on the identification and utilization of various environmental and design criteria, this book provides information that will enable the reader to construct an environmentally sensitive and visually pleasing earth-sheltered landscape.

1

Historical Overview

THE ENERGY CRISIS came to the forefront because of the 1973 oil embargo, but energy conservation, alternative ways of meeting energy needs, and the use of natural elements as energy sources are not new concepts. The only difference between today's energy-saving ideas and those of the past are the technological advances in equipment and techniques. Basic principles known and used thousands of years ago are simply being rediscovered, reapplied, and refined today.

The following brief overview of energy-related historical events illustrates the point that we are simply refining ideas that have always been used. The survey is not all-inclusive but does demonstrate that today's concepts are not new but are really variations of old ones. The survey also shows that the newly discovered ideas we have been compelled to incorporate have been forced upon us by our earlier decision to ignore the implications of rising energy costs.

8000 B.C.—Caves

Early man often lived in caves—the first earth-sheltered houses. He discovered that, along with the general protection offered by a cave, the interior temperature remained relatively constant compared to the fluctuations that occurred outside the cave (fig. 1–1). Remains of early Ice Age people were recently found in a cave in the Waco, Texas, area. Along with them were the charred bones of animals hunted by these cave dwellers, indicating man was using fire as an energy source for heat, light, and cooking.

250 A.D.—Forum Baths

The Forum Baths of Ostia in Rome combined direct-solar-gain heating with an early form of radiant heating. Sunlight was allowed to enter the structure for direct heating of the baths, and fireplaces were used to supplement the solar gain. The fireplace flues were placed in the wall and floor cavities, heating both and helping further to heat the structure.

800 A.D.—Underground Chambers

In Cappadocia, Turkey, inhabitants carved out background chambers in the soft rock, an example of earth sheltered living.

900 A.D.—Wind Power

Wind power was used in Persia to help grind grain. Windmills were first widely used at this time.

1700s—Tree Ordinance

The city of Philadelphia enacted a health regulation that recognized the intensity of the sun's heat. It required the planting of trees in the

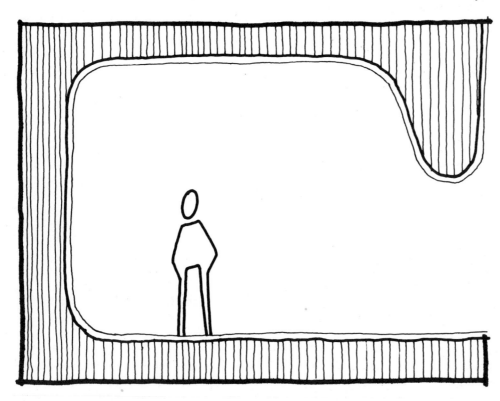

1–1. The cave—earliest form of earth sheltered dwelling.

city and said in part:

> . . . every owner or inhabitant of any and every house in Philadelphia, Newcastle, and Chester shall plant one or more tree [or] trees, *viz.,* pines, unbearing mulberries, water poplars, lime or other shady and wholesome trees before the door of his, her or their house and houses, not exceeding eight feet from the front of the house, and preserving the same, to the end that said town may be well shaded from the violence of the sun in the heat of summer and thereby rendered more healthy.

1700s—Lavoisier Lenses

The French scientist Antoin Lavoisier (1743-1794) used a series of lenses that progressively concentrated the intensity of the sun's rays until it created temperatures sufficient for the smelting of metals. The concentrated sunlight caused furnace temperatures to reach 3,000 degrees F. (1,650 degrees C.).

1800s—Sod Houses

The sod houses built in the American Midwest by many pioneering families were an early form of earth-sheltered housing (fig. 1–2). They were not warm and cozy as many people today may think. In fact, without the warmth provided by the fireplaces, they were quite uncomfortable dwellings. Since soil itself is a poor insulator the houses were not well insulated, but they did provide shelter in an otherwise unsurvivable landscape. The mass provided by the sod houses contributed to temperature moderation, and the proper southern orientation of windows, doors, and other openings also contributed to the overall efficiency. However, pioneers considered sod houses temporary shelters to be abandoned when a permanent shelter made of wood or stone was constructed.

1800s—Windmills

Over six million windmills were sold in the United States in the middle of the nineteenth century (fig. 1–3). They were used extensively in Midwestern agricultural areas, primarily to pump water out of wells and occasionally to generate electricity.

Almost all of the six million are now gone or abandoned. The cheap energy that made urban energy-usage patterns change also caused massive changes in the rural areas. Rural electric cooperatives brought all of the modern conveniences that cheap electricity could provide to the farm, and soon electricity rather than wind was used to pump water.

1800s—Firewood

Until the mid-1800s, 90 percent of the energy needs in the United States were met by the use of firewood.

1872—Street Trees

A report issued by the New York City Commissioner of Health recommended that the Department of Parks be empowered and required to plant and maintain street trees throughout the city to reduce the intense summer heat.

1890s—Geothermal Energy

The towns of Klamath Falls, Oregon, and Boise, Idaho, started using geothermal (the internal heat of the earth) hot water to heat some of the homes of their communities during the 1890s and have continued the practice to this day. Their systems have been expanded to include some municipal and state buildings as well as additional residences.

1–2. Sod houses were this country's first earth-sheltered homes.

1-3. Windmills—six million were sold but few remain active today.

1900s—Basements

In the early 1900s basements began routinely to be included in the construction of new houses (fig. 1-4).

1904—Geothermal Energy

Geothermal energy was first used in 1904 in Laderello, Italy, to generate electricity.

1909—Solar Hot Water

An engineer named William J. Bailey of Monrovia, California, patented a solar hot-water system. He used a separate collector and storage system. Before his invention, some simple solar hot-water systems were on the market in the 1890s, especially in southern California. Bailey used a thermosyphonic system—using natural temperature differences in the storage tank to move the water—rather than pumps and the pressure of incoming cold water. Storage tanks were located above the collector and he relied on the fact that colder, hence heavier water naturally sinks. It would then flow down to the collector and force the water already heated in the collector to rise to the storage tank. Likewise, warmer water is lighter than cold, and the heated water in the collector would tend naturally to rise, causing it to move to the storage tank and forcing the cooler water in the tank to flow to the collector (fig. 1-5). Bailey's business and others like his were successful until the 1920s, when oil and natural gas became readily and inexpensively available.

1922—Wind Generators

The Jacobs Wind Electric Company, Inc., was founded. Its first systems, which used wind to generate electricity, were produced during the midtwenties.

1930—Oil

A barrel of unrefined oil cost 50 cents (fig. 1-6).

1933—Chicago World's Fair

The Crystal House erected for the Chicago World's Fair was a glass-and-steel structure built to test the aesthetic combination of those two

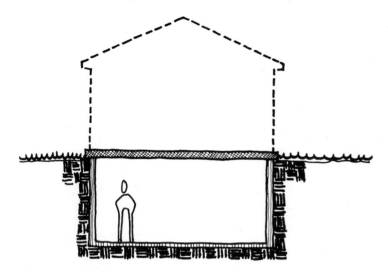

1-4. Basements became a standard part of house construction early in this century.

1-5. A simple thermosyphonic collector and storage tank system was patented in the early 1900s.

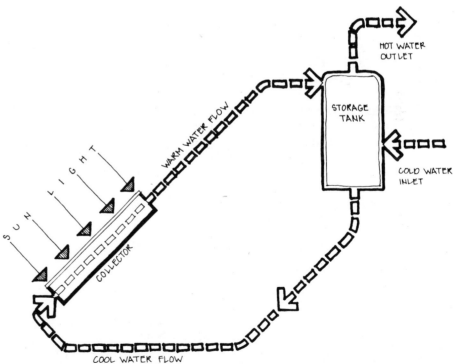

HOT WATER OUTLET

STORAGE TANK

COLD WATER INLET

WARM WATER FLOW

S U N L I G H T

COLLECTOR

COOL WATER FLOW

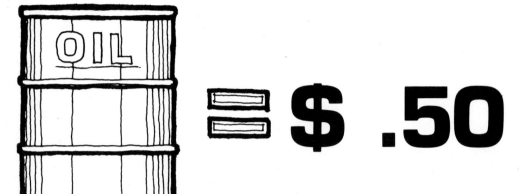

1-6. A barrel of oil cost fifty cents in 1930.

materials. The designers discovered that it was well heated by sunlight, an unplanned but welcomed result of the design.

1937-1941—Solar Hot Water

80 percent of the homes built in Miami, Florida, between 1937 and 1941 had solar hot-water heating systems (fig. 1-7). However, World War II caused a shortage of the copper used in these systems and few new ones were built. The subsequent postwar boom encouraged the development of utility companies, and their inexpensive energy production made electric water heating cheap and easy.

1939—Oil

Home heating oil cost 5.5 cents per gallon.

1940—Firewood

20 percent of the United States still used wood as the primary means of space heating.

1940s—Frank Lloyd Wright

Architect Frank Lloyd Wright designed an earth-sheltered house in Madison, Wisconsin, in the early 1940s. He used many of the ideas developed during the previous fifty years to reduce the impact of Madison's harsh winter climate (7,730 Degree Days with extreme lows

documented to minus 40 degrees F.). Wright called the structure the Solar Hemicycle.

The semicircular house was sheltered on the north side by an earth berm that reached not quite to the roof. Some narrow windows were installed along this side. Earth berming also ran along the east and west sides of the house. Here the berms sloped down to the south, which allowed the southern facade to be fully exposed to the sun. The first floor was eighteen inches below southern ground level. Slightly away from the 48-by-14-foot-high glazing on the south was a sunken area used as an outdoor space. Because of the combination of these factors—north-side earth berming, the semicircular shape of the house, and the sunken area along the south side—there was little winter wind along the house's southern face. In addition, Wright had designed the roof overhangs to prevent the summer sun from penetrating the house but to allow the lower-angled winter sun to penetrate deeply. Although Wright is given credit for many architectural innovations, few people are aware of his understanding and use of both passive-solar and earth-sheltering concepts.   •

1941—Wind Generator

The first large-scale wind generator built and operated in the United States was constructed in 1941 near Rutland, Vermont. This experimental wind-turbine generator operated intermittently for three and one-half years. It generated 1.2 million watts, which it fed to a power utility network. When the structure suffered some damage that led to a rotor failure, the utility company involved decided not to repair it. The cost of the project could not be justified, since fossil fuel could generate the same energy as the wind turbine and by that time had become less expensive.

1946—Oil

After World War II people converted home heating systems from coal and wood to oil furnaces. Oil was inexpensive, plentifully available, and, with the then-new technology, clean and easy to use (fig. 1–8).

1946—Basement Homes

G.I.s returned home to a country desperately in need of housing, especially for the many newly formed families. Many found the so-called basement homes a solution to their housing problems (fig. 1–9). These were inexpensive, partially completed homes that were exactly what their name implied, just basements. They provided immediate shelter for the veterans and their families, and could be completed as income increased. These basement homes were a form of earth-sheltered housing.

1949–1951—Lithospheric Living Spaces

"Lithospheric living spaces" was a euphemism for improved basement-type living spaces created by the combined efforts of *House Beautiful* magazine and the American Institute of Architects. The aim was to improve usually overlooked basements into climate controlled, comfortable living spaces in existing and proposed homes. This typically resulted in the ubiquitous basement level "family room" or "rumpus room," with its wood paneling, tile floor, and low ceiling. "Lithospheric living space"—basements—were actually earth-sheltered spaces.

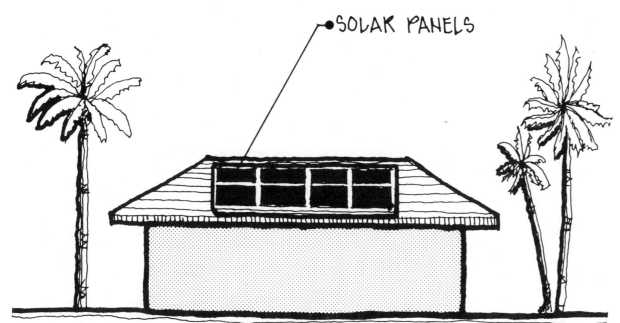

●SOLAR PANELS

1-7. Miami homes.

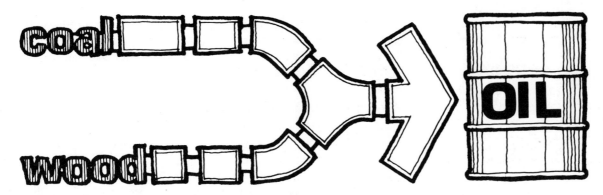

1-8. Post-World War II technology caused people to convert from coal and wood to oil-fired furnaces in their homes.

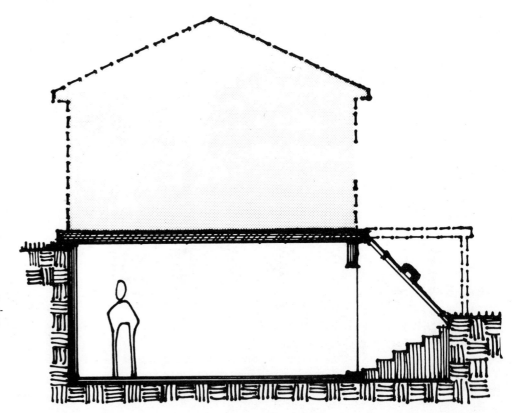

1-9. Basement homes—the answer to the returning World War II G.I.'s housing problem. Build the basement and live in it until later when the rest of the house could be afforded.

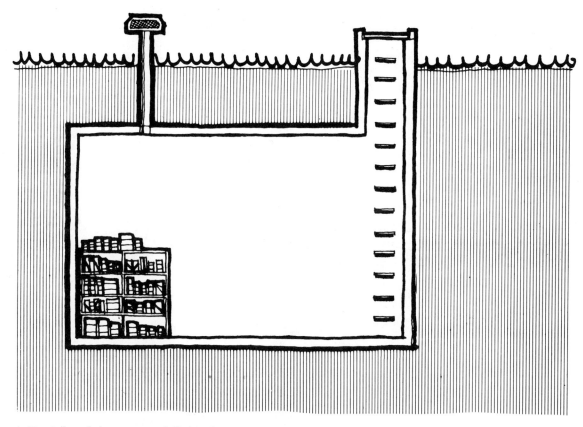

1-10. Fallout shelters were earth-sheltered structures.

1950s—Fallout Shelters

The Cold War of the 1950s caused many people to construct a different type of earth-sheltered structure: the fallout or bomb shelter. Typically these were completely underground, windowless, concrete boxes built to give a family a place to survive and live in case of atomic attack. They were often well stocked with all the supplies necessary to survive an extended stay. They were also usually cool, dark, and musty—anything but an inviting environment (fig. 1-10).

1950s—Basement Homes

The temporary basement homes built by returning World War II veterans did not always evolve into finished houses. Most communities began enacting ordinances banning their further construction (fig. 1-11).

1954—Photovoltaic Cells

Photovoltaic cells, which produce electricity from solar radiation,

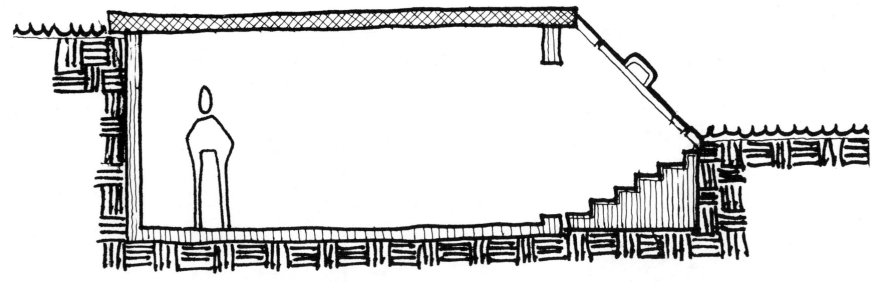

1–11. Basement homes often remained basements and were never completed.

1–12. Photovoltaics—the space program uses cells to generate the electricity needed for space vehicles.

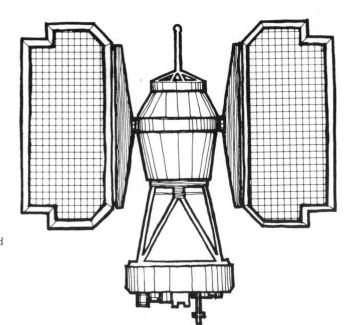

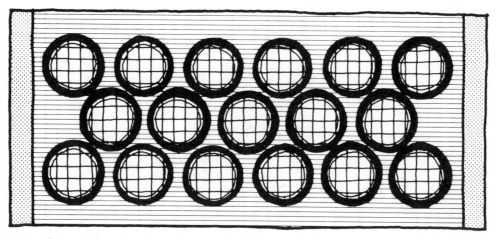

1-13. Photovoltaics—solar cells are improving in efficiency and reducing in cost.

were first produced by Bell Laboratories in 1954. They were tremendously expensive to make, and few uses were found for them until the space program in the early 1960s. Since that time, much of the electricity used on space equipment, from the first satellites to today's extended space flights, has been produced by such cells (fig. 1–12). As cell-construction technology has improved and the cost of the fuels that the cells might replace has increased, the actual cost of the cells has come down (fig. 1–13).

1960—Wind Generators

Because of federal subsidies for rural electrification programs and other economic factors, the Jacobs Wind Electric Company was forced to close its wind-generator business.

1965—Malcolm Wells

Progressive Architecture magazine published an article by architect Malcolm Wells entitled "Nowhere to Go But Down," in which he described earth-sheltered structures and discussed their benefits.

1970s—Photovoltaic Cells

The camera industry incorporated a photovoltaic-cell system into the camera to create an extremely sensitive and highly accurate light meter (fig. 1–14).

1970—Barrel of Oil

The price of oil from OPEC (Organization of Petroleum Exporting Countries) was less than two dollars per barrel (fig. 1–15).

1971—Firewood

Because of the inexpensive and readily available fossil fuels, less than one percent of the energy needs in the United States were supplied by wood.

Pre–1973—Pre-embargo Earth-sheltered Structures

Before the 1973 oil embargo, many earth-sheltered structures were built as a response to the environmental movement of the late sixties and early seventies. Some designers, led by landscape architects, believed that structures all too often seemed imposed upon the landscape rather than integrated into the site. Earth sheltering was one response to that belief. With the 1973 embargo, however, earth sheltering gained a new, more immediate rationale—conservation of energy and energy dollars.

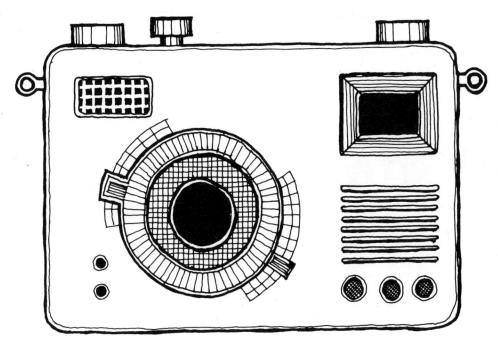

1-14. The camera industry used photovoltaic technology to produce cameras with accurate and sensitive light meters built in.

1-15. In 1970, the cost of a barrel of oil reached two dollars per barrel, an all-time high.

 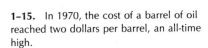 **$2.00**

Dec.,1973

Jan.,1973

1-16. 1973—the year of the OPEC oil embargo and a quadrupling of oil prices.

1973—Oil Embargo

The first major embargo of oil occurred in 1973. The people of the United States were suddenly awakened to their energy vulnerability. They were forced for the first time to pay energy costs similar to those paid by the citizens of many European countries.

1973—Barrel of Oil

The price of oil from OPEC was less than three dollars per barrel in January 1973 and almost twelve dollars by December 1973 (Fig. 1–16).

1973—Oil Imports

In 1973 the United States imported 36 percent of its oil requirements.

1973—Wind Generators

With electric costs escalating and the possibility of energy shortages, the Jacobs Wind Electric Company began new research and development. Later in the decade it actually renewed production of wind generators.

Post-1973—Gasohol

Gasohol is a mixture of 90 percent gasoline and 10 percent ethanol, an alcohol typically produced from corn. It was promoted as a means of reducing the total dependence on oil products and as well to create more of a demand for locally producible energy material (fig. 1–17). In the first half of 1979, motorists in the state of Iowa alone purchased 28 million gallons of gasohol.

1974—Insulation

The average R-value in the ceiling of a new home in the United States was 17.9, and in the walls 10.2.

1977—Oil Imports

Imported oil accounted for almost 50 percent of the oil usage in the United States.

1978—Natural Gas

The United States Congress passed the Natural Gas Policy Act, which began the process of removing government-imposed price con-

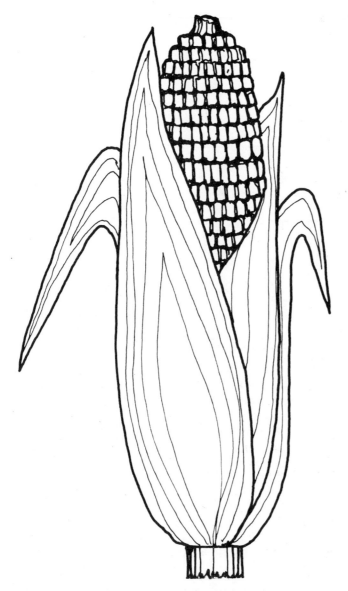

1-17. Gasohol is a mixture of alcohol and gasoline. It is only one of the uses of corn alcohol but perhaps the best known.

trols on natural gas. The act was seen as a means of both rationing and extending limited natural-gas reserves.

1978—Earth-sheltered House

The Underground Space Center at the University of Minnesota published its first book on the basics of earth-sheltered houses. More than 4,000 copies were sold in the first three weeks that it was available.

1978—Insulation

The average R-value in the ceiling of a new home in the United States was 24.3, and in the walls 11.5.

1978—Gasohol

The State of Iowa established a different gas-tax rate for gasohol. The pump price for gasohol became less than that for straight gasoline.

1978—Sun Day

On May 3, 1978, there was a national celebration of the world's only inexhaustible, predictable, egalitarian, nonpolluting, safe, terrorist-resistant, and free energy source. It was called Sun Day (fig. 1–19).

1979—Energy Sources

Almost 48 percent of the total energy used in the United States came from oil, and about 25 percent came from natural gas. It is estimated that by the year 2000, those numbers will be 30 percent and 20 percent respectively. This predicted reduction was seen as a response to the diminishing supply of oil and natural gas, and the concurrent increase in cost, leading to a situation where fewer and fewer households would be able to afford these fuels.

1979—Earth-sheltered House

The Underground Space Center's book had sold nearly 70,000 copies by mid-1979, mostly through word-of-mouth advertising.

1980s—Basement Homes

The zoning ordinances and building codes enacted over the past thirty years to prevent the construction of basement homes were interpreted to prevent the construction of earth-sheltered homes.

1980—Building Codes

The State of Wisconsin adopted a new state building code that

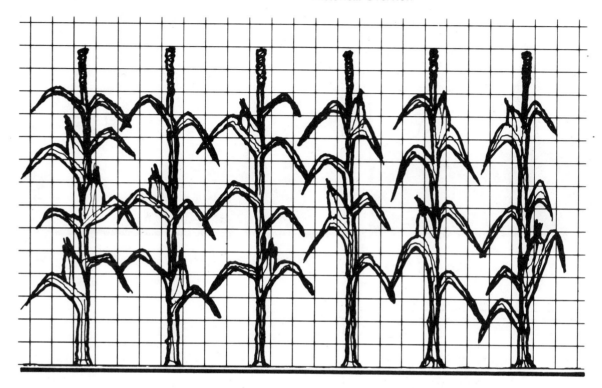

1-18. An acre of corn (100 bushels) holds 38 million Btus in its grain and an additional 50 million Btus in its stalks, leaves, and cobs.

recognized the unique construction characteristics of underground structures. The code did not eliminate safety and light requirements of the more traditional-building codes but did address underground structures in particular and applied certain interpretations unique to earth-sheltered design.

1980—Firewood

With the advent of expensive fuels, wood began to be looked at as a less costly energy source. Wood now supplied almost 2 percent of United States energy needs and the percentage was growing every day (fig. 1-20).

1981—Gasohol

More than 30 million gallons of gasohol were sold in the State of Iowa during the month of December.

1983—Solar Power

The rock group Styx claimed to be the first music group to use solar power to record music. They recorded an album in a Chicago studio using a solar-powered generator.

1983—Barrel of Oil

OPEC cut the cost of a barrel of oil by five dollars, dropping the price from thirty-four dollars to twenty-nine dollars per barrel on March 14. It was the first reduction in price ever for the twenty-three-year-old organization, brought about by the threat of a global price war and a worldwide excess of currently available oil.

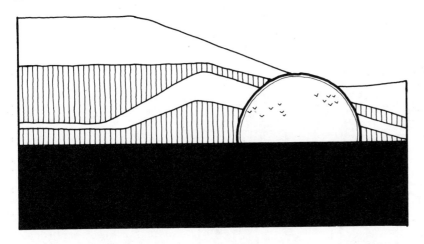

1-19. Sun Day, May 3, 1978.

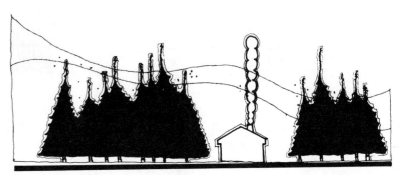

1-20. In 1976, over 6 percent of New England's homes were heated totally with wood.

1-21. In 1983, the price of a barrel of oil "drops" to only twenty-nine dollars, down from 1981's high of thirty-four dollars.

2

Earth Shelter: Context

AN ENERGY CRISIS exists in the United States, and the country's 80 million wall thermostats are partially responsible for creating this crisis. The thermostats have allowed us to substitute fossil fuels for climate-responsive structures. Rather than orient windows and doors away from cold winter winds, we have simply learned to turn up the thermostat. Rather than understand how the sun might be used to warm our homes, we have had only to understand how to adjust the setting on the wall thermostat. Until the seventies, we had little concern for and, in fact, little awareness of the consequences of all those adjustments.

Today we are acutely aware. We realize that there is a tremendous cost consequence involved when we change the thermostat and, more likely than not, we find ourselves lowering the winter setting rather than raising it as we would have in the past. We now conserve and minimize our use of all energy sources because it is too costly not to do so.

Electricity, oil, coal, natural gas, and other energy sources have dramatically risen in cost since the oil crises of the seventies. Home energy costs have skyrocketed whereas actual consumption has dropped (fig. 2-1). Electricity and natural gas, two of the most common home energy sources, have been chasing each other up the ever-increasing cost spiral at a rate that frightens even the people most able to afford to pay the higher costs. For those on limited incomes, energy cost increases may mean that there will not be enough money to cover basic monthly expenses.

The increased energy cost that affects us most directly is that of our home's energy. Space heating—keeping warm in the winter—is the primary energy expense in a home (fig. 2-2).

Many homes use fossil fuels directly for space heating. Others use electricity. However, most electrically heated homes are indirectly consuming fossil fuels as well, because more than 90 percent of this nation's electricity is generated from heat obtained by burning oil, coal, or natural gas. Thus, all the usual forms of space heating are great consumers of fossil fuel.

The fact that heating is the primary use of energy is documented by the following summary of one midwestern state's 1981 typical home energy consumption:

Space Heating	75.0 percent
Water Heating	9.5
Air Conditioning	6.0
Lights and Appliances	9.5

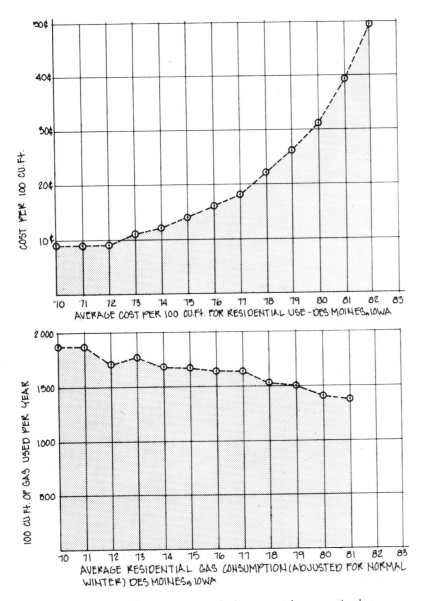

2-1. Home energy costs have skyrocketed whereas actual consumption has dropped.

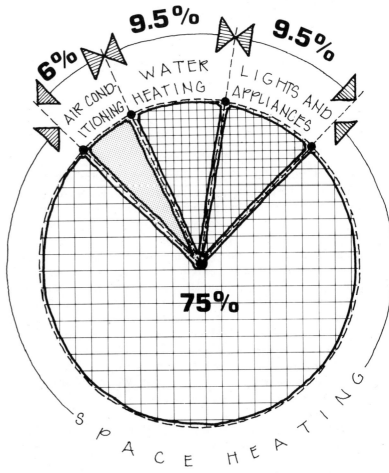

2-2. Home energy use in a typical Iowa home, 1983.

Three-quarters of the energy expended in an average household was used to keep the house warm. That figure explains why even the smallest improvement in the energy efficiency of the house can have a significant effect on the total energy costs for that house. Energy dollars can be saved today in existing structures by adding insulation, caulking windows, lowering hot-water-heater temperatures, and turning off unnecessary lights. These measures do not have the glamour that constructing a new energy-efficient building might have, but they do much to reduce energy costs in existing structures (fig. 2–3).

The idea of constructing a new home, however, is very much a consideration for people now living in energy-inefficient housing. The ever-increasing cost of heating a home has led to interest in active-solar, passive-solar, and earth-sheltered housing.

A certain mystique has grown with the newfound awareness of the energy-saving ability of earth-sheltered structures, as well as some misconceptions. New construction plans should be based on strictly factual criteria. The following are some reasons to use earth-sheltering techniques, especially in housing.

1.   The two main causes of heat loss in a house are *heat transfer,* heat escaping through the walls and ceilings through the process of

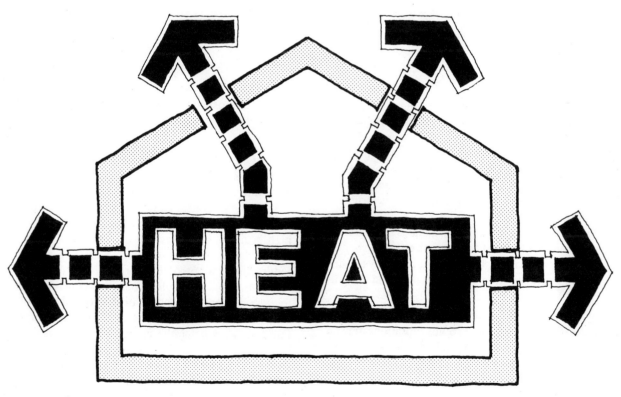

2–3. According to Department of Energy estimates, some 40 million single-family homes are not adequately protected from outside weather.

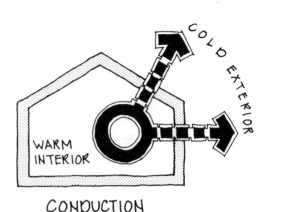

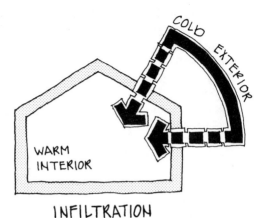

2-4. Heat loss in a house primarily results from conduction, heat moving from the warm interior to the cold exterior, and infiltration, the movement of cold outside air into the structure through cracks and other openings.

2-5. Earth sheltering helps isolate the interior from exterior noise.

conduction, and *infiltration,* the uncontrolled movement of air into and out of the structure (fig. 2-4). The energy-saving ability of an earth-sheltered structure is based on the ability of soil covering to minimize infiltration and to reduce the problem of conduction.

Infiltration is minimized because its cause, wind, is separated from the structure by the covering of earth. Without direct contact between walls and wind, outside air cannot force itself into the structure through the tiny openings typically found in an above-ground wall. Conduction is reduced since the covering of earth isolates the extremes of exterior temperature from the walls of the structure. Earth sheltering does not take the place of insulation, but it goes a long way toward reducing heat loss by minimizing the effects of conduction and infiltration.

2.   The interiors of earth-sheltered structures tend to be quiet since the surrounding earth muffles exterior noises. Some vibrations may be transmitted, but most sounds are lost or absorbed before they can reach the structure (fig. 2-5).

3.   Since most earth-sheltered structures are constructed with concrete, concrete block, other masonry, or stone, they tend to be more fire resistant, rot resistant, and even pest resistant if constructed prop-

erly, than most conventional structures. In addition, storm damage is less likely because of the construction techniques and the earth covering.

4.   One of the inherent design problems in any passive-solar building is finding a means of incorporating adequate quantities of mass into the construction. Mass here is any material that can be used to store the solar heat gained by a passive-solar building. Typically, the mass material is masonry, although it can be water or other suitable high heat storage capacity—high thermal conductive material (table 2-1). Increasing the amount of mass in a structure will, in general, reduce the amount of temperature fluctuation within the structure. Whereas wood, particularly oak, and concrete have similar heat capacity, wood does not conduct heat well and is not commonly used as a thermal mass material. Generally, the more thermal mass the better. Further, the greater the amount of thermal mass exposed to direct sunlight, the smaller the fluctuation in internal space temperature.

The "mass" construction techniques of the adobe structures built by the native Indians in the southwestern United States are a good example of how thermal mass reduces temperature fluctuation. These adobe structures use their tremendous mass to temper the effect of the wide temperature fluctuations in the outer environment. The exterior walls absorb enormous amounts of sunshine and, were it not for the large amount of mass, the heat generated by that absorption would soon overheat the interior. Because of the thickness of the exterior wall, the heat moves slowly through the wall inch by inch. Each successive layer of the wall must first change temperature before passing excess thermal energy on to the next layer, and this slow process impedes the heat flow. The result is that, while the outdoor temperature may fluctuate, the indoor temperature remains relatively stable.

Table 2-1 Thermal characteristics of various materials

Material	Specific Heat	Density	Heat Capacity
Water	1.000	62.400	62.400
Wood (Oak)	0.570	47.000	26.800
Wood (Pine)	0.330	32.000	10.600
Air	0.240	0.075	0.018
Brick	0.200	123.000	25.000
Concrete*	0.270	140.000	38.000
Concrete*	0.156	144.000	22.000

* Note: Different sources list different figures for these materials.

The *heat storage ability* of a material is measured by its *specific heat* (the number of Btus required to raise one pound of the material one degree F.). The higher the number, the more heat energy storage ability the material has.
Density is a measure of the weight of one cubic foot of the material (pounds per cubic foot).
Heat Capacity is a measure of the material's heat storage capacity:

specific heat × density = heat capacity.

Earth-sheltered structures in general tend to have mass components as an integral part of the building. The mass within an earth-sheltered structure tempers the effect of large amounts of sunlight entering a structure by absorbing the excess thermal energy for later use. The masonry walls, ceilings, and floors typical to many earth-sheltered construction techniques are an important, built-in part of the necessary thermal-mass system.

5. Earth-sheltered structures can save energy dollars. They are naturally warmer in the winter and cooler in the summer than their non-earth-sheltered counterparts, as stated in point one. However, total net energy-dollar savings can be adversely affected by the site location (as discussed in chapter 4).

It is also important to note that the energy savings possible with an earth-sheltered structure are not only monetary. The lowered consumption of energy also reduces the use of nonrenewable resources.

Enthusiasm for the earth-sheltered concept needs to be tempered with the realization of just what an earth-sheltered structure is and is not. There is no current standard definition of "earth-sheltered." However, whenever the term "earth-sheltered house" is used, everyone has an image of what the term describes (fig. 2-6). Without fail, those images are of a building covered with earth, one that is radically different from a "standard" home built in any subdivision across the United States. However, buildings should not be classified as "earth-sheltered" or "not earth sheltered." Rather, they should be looked at in terms of how much earth sheltering occurs. Many structures are somewhat earth-sheltered and many so-called conventional structures are at least partially earth-sheltered structures (fig. 2-7).

The standard basement built as a part of most homes since the turn of the century is a type of earth-sheltered structure (fig. 2-8). The basement walls are indeed "sheltered" by surrounding soil, and the basement environment is protected from the radical fluctuations in outside air temperatures with which the "above ground" portion of the structure must contend. The common "walkout basement" is simply an earth-sheltered structure, covered on three sides by earth, with a conventional above-ground structure built over it.

The common split-foyer home found in most suburban developments is also a type of earth-sheltered structure (fig. 2.9). The lower level of the split is typically four to five feet below the surrounding soil level and therefore earth-sheltered. Underground parking ramps, subways, garden apartments, and countless other everyday structures can all be considered somewhat earth-sheltered. It is important to remember that most structures are earth-sheltered to some degree and that earth sheltering is not an either-or situation.

That most structures are somewhat earth-sheltered is related to the fact that most structures can be considered passive-solar to some degree as well. "Passive solar" does not describe a type of architec-

2-6. When people see the term "earth-sheltered," they often visualize a structure with soil piled up to the roof line, as shown here, or even soil on the roof. (Photograph by Rod Stevens. Courtesy Green Meadows Ltd.)

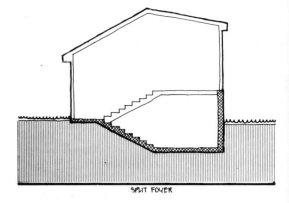

SPLIT FOYER

2-7. Many so-called conventional structures are forms of earth-sheltered buildings.

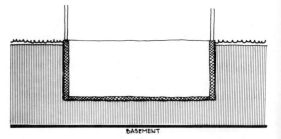

BASEMENT

Section

2-8. Earth-sheltering does not always mean the building up of soil along the walls of a structure. The bedroom level of this house, for instance, is earth-sheltered as a result of the house being lowered into the site rather than the site being built up around the house. Some earth-sheltering is accomplished on the kitchen's north wall by building up a small amount of soil, but the sheltering of the bedroom level is accomplished by lowering the house beneath the natural grade of this essentially flat site. The zone just south of the southern bedroom wall has been excavated to allow both light and air to reach the bedrooms. (Drawing courtesy Green Meadows Ltd.)

2-9. Note the excavated area on the far left of this photograph. It allows the low winter sun to enter the below – grade, earth-sheltered bedroom windows. (Photograph by Rod Stevens. Courtesy Green Meadows Ltd.)

ture; it describes a means of using the energy in sunlight. The words simply imply that an object receives some of its energy needs (typically direct-heat-gain) from sunshine.

Every structure that allows sunshine to penetrate its interior can be considered passive-solar. Probably 99 percent of the homes in the United States allow sunshine to enter so each of them can be thought of as passive-solar. Some are designed to capture and use that gain more efficiently than others. The more efficient ones are those typically called passive-solar homes.

If active-solar systems are defined as solar-collection systems that use mechanical means of concentrating, capturing, storing, or dispersing solar energy, then most passive-solar homes are active-solar homes as well. While some passive-solar homes may use simple nonmechanical thermosyphoning techniques to move air warmed by passive-collection means, many use small fans, electric shutters, or other mechanical devices to move or control interior temperatures. Even less directly passive-solar homes, the so-called traditional structures, may in the winter use the furnace fan alone without the furnace heating system to help circulate the heat gained from whatever south-facing windows exist.

The concepts of earth-sheltered, passive-solar, and active-solar homes presented here are intended to demonstrate that really very little is magical or mysterious about those concepts. The ideas are not radical departures from what is currently being constructed and called conventional. What we typically call earth-sheltered, passive-solar, active-solar, or energy-efficient housing is simply housing that has incorporated and expanded upon certain design concepts that make them more energy-efficient than other houses.

Earth-sheltered houses, for instance, take the basement or split-foyer idea a bit further and cover even more of the structure with soil. Passive-solar homes simply maximize southern glass, minimize all other glass, incorporate heat-storing mass, and use solar energy to provide some direct heat for the home. Active-solar homes go beyond the simple furnace-fan assist and often use complicated mechanical methods of capturing, storing, and distributing solar energy.

Earth-sheltered-home designers typically and logically incorporate passive-solar concepts into the design. Although the homes do not have to be passive-solar (they can in fact be oriented away from the sun), common sense dictates that earth-sheltered structures use good solar orientation (fig. 2–10). More traditional active-solar systems such as solar panels or photocells may also be incorporated into earth-sheltered homes. Again, the active components are not necessary for the house to be energy-efficient, but they may add to the overall energy efficiency.

In 1976, fewer than fifty earth-sheltered homes existed. In 1978, fifty were under construction. By 1983 there were 3,000 to 4,000 earth-sheltered homes in use. Today, it is estimated that twice that number (7,000 to 8,000) are built or being built and the demand continues to be strong.

Earth-sheltered homes are not a fad that will pass. They are a logical outgrowth of our concerns for saving energy and energy costs while still providing the basic shelter we all need. The planning and design of earth-sheltered homes will continue, and each refinement will contribute to the overall quality, efficiency, and aesthetics of the homes that are built.

2-10. Earth-sheltered, passive solar, and an active-solar rooftop panel all contribute to the energy efficiency of this house. (Photograph by Rod Stevens. Courtesy of Green Meadows Ltd.)

3

Natural Elements I: Vegetation and Land

A S STATED PREVIOUSLY, countless environmental influences affect the energy efficiency of a structure. This chapter will discuss some of these basic influences.

Vegetation, sun, wind, and the land in general are all parts of that influencing environment. Some understanding of the nature of each of these influences is necessary in order to know how they affect a structure. It is also important to establish common definitions and create a common vocabulary with which to discuss each element.

The following sections discuss various aspects of the basic natural elements, first on a detailed level with vegetation and land, then on a more cursory level with sun and wind. Like all other parts of the environment that are linked, the discussion of any one element always includes other elements. The somewhat arbitrary separation in this chapter allows us to direct the discussion toward earth-sheltered landscapes and to prepare for the following chapters on site selection and site planning.

VEGETATION

Vegetation is obviously an important part of our discussion of earth-sheltered landscapes. Plants are the basic design materials of any landscape, and their proper use can mean the difference between a pleasing, functional site and one that is not. The functional design aspects of vegetation and other site features are discussed in the following chapters on site selection and site planning. The important vegetation information presented here addresses the various life forms of plant material, some basic ecological principles, a discussion of vegetation and energy, and information on vegetation as a sound barrier and environmental indicator.

Forms of Vegetation

Vegetation can be separated and classified in many different ways. Technical systems are used to identify individual plant species, but these systems are not necessary in this discussion of earth-sheltered landscapes. What does need to be established, however, is a standard vocabulary for separating plants into broad categories based on the size of the plant and on whether the plant is evergreen or deciduous. Landscape architects tend to use some variation of the system shown in figure 3–1. The sketches show the physical appearance of each of the plant forms that are discussed in the chapter on site planning.

Overstory Trees   These are plants that grow well above eye level and form the overhead canopy layer of vegetation. The group may in-

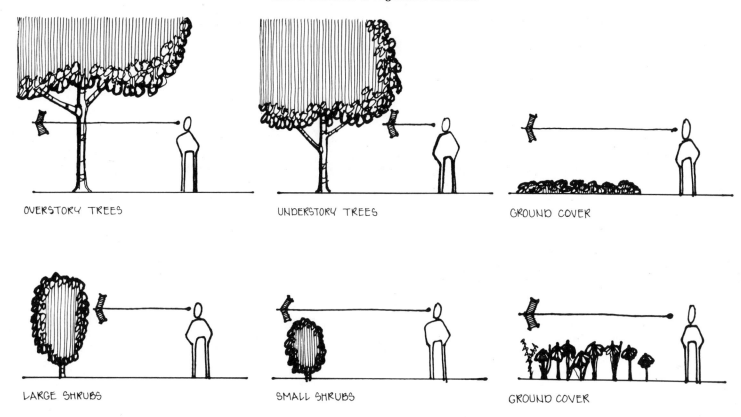

OVERSTORY TREES   UNDERSTORY TREES   GROUND COVER

LARGE SHRUBS   SMALL SHRUBS   GROUND COVER

3–1. Forms of vegetation.

clude some of the larger fruit trees as well as the more typically thought of oaks, maples, ashes, and pines.

Understory Trees   These may have lower branches at eye level but they also may form part of the overhead canopy. The smaller fruit trees, as well as plants such as hawthorns, flowering dogwoods, and redbuds, should be included in this category.

Shrubs   The division between tall shrubs and small trees is sometimes vague, but it is not a critical issue. Shrubs are usually at, just above, or just below eye level and can form barriers, direct views, and control movement in a landscape. It is a very broad category that includes azaleas, dogwoods, junipers, and yews. Many plants not typically thought of as landscaping plants should also be included in this category, such as raspberries, blueberries, and other garden shrubs.

Ground Cover   This group of plants covers a wide range of vegetation, all of which typically occur below eye level. The category has traditionally been limited, especially in earth-sheltered landscapes, to turf grass. It can, however, be so much more diverse with a little imagination. Beyond the common ground covers such as periwinkle and

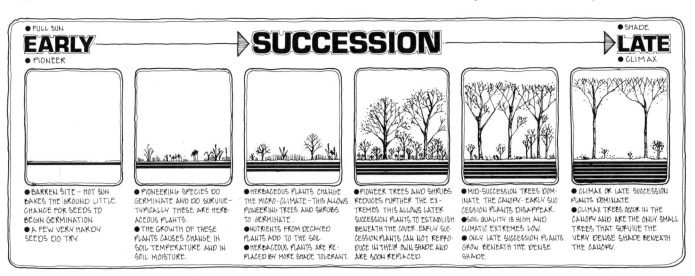

3-2. *Succession.* Typical upper midwestern continuum from early succession to climax vegetation.

wintercreeper, there are many vines, wildflowers, ferns, garden plants, annuals, perennials, and small plants that too often are overlooked as possible ground-cover plants.

Vegetation—Basic Ecological Principles

Three basic ecological principles need to be addressed in this discussion of earth-sheltered landscapes. They are succession, adaptation, and diversity.

Succession   In simplistic terms, *succession* could be described as the following of or replacement of one group of plants by another group of plants. In actuality, succession describes a complex evolutionary process for any group of plants or plant community. The evolution is usually from an early-succession (or pioneering) community to a late-succession (or climax) community. At each point in the process there is a specific group of plants suited to all of the microclimatic conditions—the surroundings—that exist at that particular site at that particular time. The change in the community—the addition and deletion of various plants from that community, that is, succession—is caused by alterations in that microclimate, and those changes are often caused

by the existing plant material themselves. The plant-induced changes include those in the soil (texture, moisture content, nutrients, pH), in light levels (full sun, partial sun, filtered sunlight, full shade) and countless other changes, each of which affect any one particular plant's chances of survival.

Early-succession plants usually require full sun and low competition from other plant material. They often are quite tolerant of particularly harsh conditions and extremes of microclimate, to the point that they may be the only plants capable of colonizing a barren site. Late-succession plants usually become established after the pioneering plants have stabilized the site and moderated the extremes. They typically grow in more shaded and/or microclimatically stable situations that are not subject to extremes.

The succession principle, like many principles in nature, is not absolutely true all the time. Situations exist where a seemingly early-succession plant will be found in a late-succession situation. Likewise, a late-succession, climax-type species may be found colonizing a barren site. However, the principle is generally valid, usually well demonstrated in naturally occurring sites, and is an appropriate guideline to use in the selection of plant material for earth-sheltered landscapes (fig. 3-2).

Adaptation   Whereas succession demonstrates the evolution of a plant community, *adaptation* is the principle that says certain plant species can be identified as typical of one or more specific microclimates. For example, if a site is a hot and dry exposed hillside, a predictable community of plant species will most likely be growing on that site. That community of plants, or at least many of the individual plants, might also be found on other sites with different types of microclimates. Ecologically, however, the individual plants, and particularly the relative mix of those plants, are most predictably found wherever that specific mix of microclimatic criteria exist.

Like succession, the adaptation principle is not an absolute. However, it too is a strong principle that should be used as part of the plant-selection process for earth-sheltered landscapes (fig. 3–3).

Diversity   The third ecological principle, *diversity,* is a measure of the range in variety or number of species found on a given site. The plant variety, given the constraints of succession and adaptation, account for the health of that plant community.

Overplanting of a single species, as with the American elm, can lead to environmental catastrophes. Street after street across the United States was planted with American elm, thus making it more vulnerable to Dutch elm disease. The spread of the disease might have been slowed and the visual effect of the trees' decimation might have been less dramatic had the elm been planted along with other species rather than in the continuous monotype (single species) fashion it was.

Diversity does not mean that every plant must be a different species than the plant next to it. Some degree of consistency is still important. What constitutes variety is a subjective decision and perhaps can be discussed only in general terms rather than in technical or numerical ways. The two graphs shown in figure 3–4 show the relationship of diversity to succession and the amount of diversity typically found in a naturally occurring plant community.

These three ecological principles, succession, adaptation, and diversity, should always be considered in the plant-selection process for

3–3. *Adaptation.* Microclimatic differences for various orientations in an upper midwestern woodland.

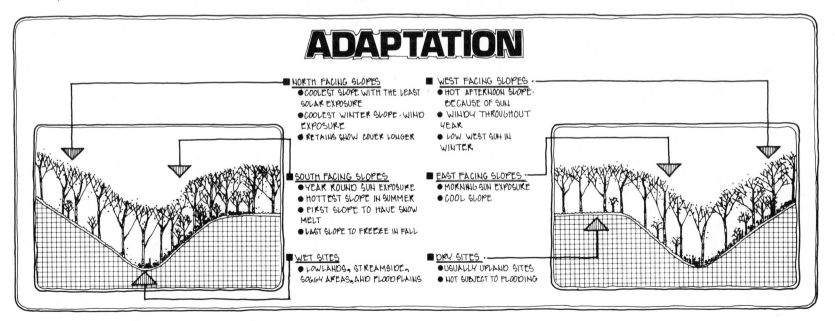

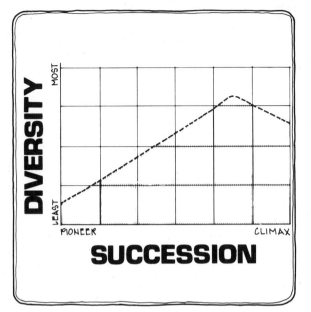

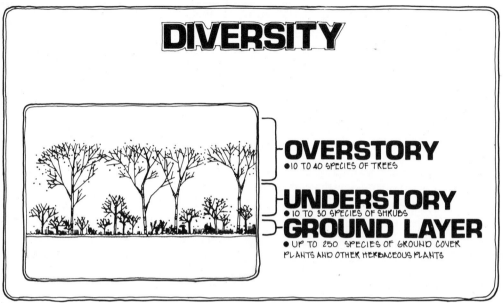

3-4. *Diversity.* Relative diversity patterns in upper midwestern ecosystems.

earth-sheltered landscapes. The result, as will be discussed later in the design chapter, will be a landscape of variety without chaos, continuity without monotony, and beauty combined with harmony.

Vegetation as Environmental Indicators

Plants that exist on a site can be used to identify past and present land uses and can help identify hidden or confirm indicated micro-habitats. Since plants have optimum habitats controlled by the quantity and quality of sunlight, water, soils, slopes, and other environmental and cultural influences, the existence of certain plants on a given site can give clues to the makeup of the site.

Some plants can be used to identify or at least speculate upon former land uses in any given area. The presence of large quantities of bull thistles (Cirsium lanceolatum) in an open, sunlit, grassy field indicates a recent history of heavy grazing. In a woodland, grazing is often in-

dicated by the excessive dominance of thorny plants like wild goose-berry (Ribes missouriense). Soils recently disturbed by man's activities or natural processes may often be identified by the large populations of common ragweed (Ambrosia artemisiifolia), giant ragweed (Ambrosia trifida), and curly dock (Rumex crispus).

The presence of some plants can suggest certain soil conditions or compositions. The various plantins (Plantago sp.) are typically found in soils compacted by foot or vehicle traffic. In the northeastern states, Eastern columbine (Aquilegia canadensis) is often associated with high limestone (calcium carbonate) presence in the soil or substrate. Eastern redbud (Cercis canadensis) is commonly found with dolomite (calcium and magnesium carbonate). Rhododendrons of the southeastern United States tend to be found in soils that have a higher than average acid level.

Cactuses indicate a dry site. Likewise, cattails would identify a wet, marshy site. In all of these examples, existence of certain plants can be used to make assumptions about each of the sites.

Other plants may not as dramatically indicate a site's condition, but knowing a plant's typical habitat can perhaps lead an investigator to some otherwise undiscoverable observations or revelations. (Watts' *Reading the Landscape* is a recommended reference.)

Vegetation and Sunlight

Sunlight is essential for plant growth and survival. It is the energy source that allows the photosynthetic process to take place (fig. 3–5). Plants need adequate amounts of sunlight, and they need the sunlight to be in a form usable by the plant.

The solar energy that strikes the earth's surface is not all absorbed by the layer of green plants on the surface. Most is scattered or reflected so that only 2 percent is actually absorbed by plants. Of that 2 percent, half is in the proper wavelength of the electromagnetic spectrum, and only that half can be combined with chlorophyll to produce stored chemical energy (fig. 3–6).

Each plant absorbs and photosynthetically uses different quantities of light energy along the 0.4-to-0.8-micron continuum of the spectrum. An individual plant has its own characteristic light-absorbing fingerprint, based upon the various identifiable bands of light energy that it absorbs or reflects.

The quantity of light that reaches the plants also influences the health of the plant material. Just as individual plants have definitive wavelength requirements, they also have certain light-quantity needs. Some plants must be exposed to full and continual sunlight and cannot survive any amount of shading. Other plants prosper in very shady situations, and for them exposure to full sun would be harmful.

Sunlight is often measured in footcandles (see table 3–1). The top leaves of a tree in a forest will receive thousands of footcandles of sunlight, while it is possible for the smallest plants on the forest floor to

$$6CO_2 + 6H_2O + \text{Light energy} + \text{Chlorophyll} = C_6H_{12}O_6 + 6O_2$$

Carbon dioxide + Water + Light + Chlorophyll =

SUGAR + OXYGEN

3–5. Photosynthetic equation.

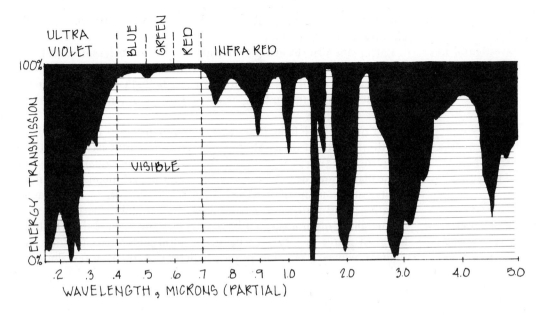

3-6. The electromagnetic spectrum.

ULTRA VIOLET BLUE GREEN RED INFRA RED

VISIBLE

% ENERGY TRANSMISSION

100%

0%

.2 .3 .4 .5 .6 .7 .8 .9 1.0 2.0 3.0 4.0 5.0

WAVELENGTH, MICRONS (PARTIAL)

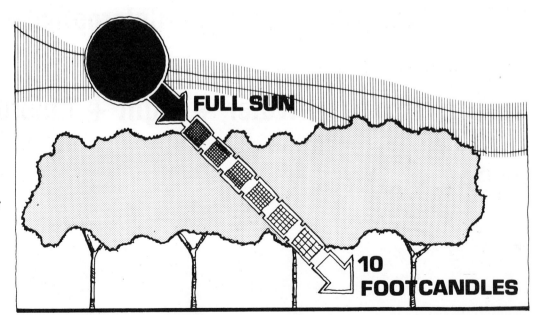

3-7. Filtered sunlight on a forest floor may be under ten footcandles, whereas the top of the forest canopy may be receiving 10,000 footcandles. The same relationship can occur in a planned landscape using overstory trees.

FULL SUN

10 FOOTCANDLES

receive less than forty footcandles and still survive (fig. 3–7). Each plant has its sunlight-quantity needs and, although it may survive under other conditions, continued health and vigor is best ensured under optimum conditions.

Plants as an Energy Source

Part of the solar energy that reaches the earth is captured by the green plants that cover the surface. The solar energy that strikes the plants is converted to stored chemical energy through the process of photosynthesis. It is this stored energy that supplies the energy needs of our shelters, vehicles, and machines. It is also the energy source used by other life forms, including human beings.

The stored chemical energy that exists in plants is supplied in many forms, and it is of many different ages (fig. 3–8). The food consumed today consists of recently captured solar energy, especially if it is the plant material itself, such as vegetables or fruit. When meat and other animal products such as milk and eggs are consumed, again they contain the energy stored in plants. Each of the animals originally received its energy from plants, whether it was grain, grass, or other vegetative sources. The stored chemical energy is released in the bodies of the con-

sumer organism (human beings, cattle, chickens, and so on) in the form of calories.

Table 3-1 Footcandle chart

		LIGHT
		LEVELS,
8000	Summer, Midday Sun, South Window	NEAR
5500	Winter, Midday Sun, South Window	
2000–4000	Winter Sun, East or West Window	GLASS
1000–2000	Cloudy Day, Midday Sun, South Window	IN
300	Sunny Winter Day, North Glass	BUILDING
		INTERIORS
200	Watchmaking	LIGHT
100	Critical Vision, Low Contrast	LEVELS
50	Prolonged Office Work	NECESSARY
30	Classrooms	FOR
20	Gymnasiums	
10	Stairways	VARIOUS
5	Corridors	TASKS

Stored Solar Energy   Age of Source

FOOD (VEGETABLE) . . . . MOST RECENT
FOOD (ANIMAL) . . . . RECENT
FIREWOOD . . . . MEASURED IN YEARS
FOSSIL FUELS . . . . MEASURED IN THOUSANDS
AND THOUSANDS OF YEARS

3–8. Plants as an energy source.

The wood burned in fireplaces and furnaces is also stored solar energy, although it is energy that was captured further in the past than in food sources (fig. 3-9). The stored chemical energy in wood is released during the combustion process, and typically is in the form of heat. Some of the energy is lost in the evaporative process, especially if the firewood has a high moisture content, but most of the energy is nonetheless released as usable heat. The effectiveness of plants as combustion-heat sources differs from species to species. The length of time and method used to cure the firewood also has a definite effect on the amount of energy received per given quantity of wood (see table 3-2). The use of firewood is common throughout the world. It is estimated that even today one-third of the earth's population is dependent on wood as its principal source of energy.

The oldest forms of stored plant-material energy are oil, coal, and gas. These exist in deposits around the world. Coal and oil originated millions of years ago as both plant and animal life, and over many thousands of years have been converted to their present form. These ancient forms are removed from the earth and used as fuels, releasing the stored solar energy that was captured so long ago. As in the burning of firewood, the stored energy in oil and coal is released typically as heat during a combustion process. Again like firewood, this heat energy may be used to generate other forms of energy, such as electricity.

Vegetation as an Energy Controller

Vegetation is a source of energy, but it is also an energy controller.

Such control occurs in many ways, from the simple providing of shade to the complex relationship between an area's vegetation and its microclimate. Vegetation can be used to lessen climatic extremes and can be utilized to accentuate the positive elements of a given climate.

Table 3-2 Relative heat value of wood at different amounts of "seasoning"

HARDWOOD SEASONING		
Condition of Wood	Heat Value (% of value for air dry)	Moisture Content (% of oven-dry weight)
Green in fall, winter, spring*	85	80
Green in summer	93	65
Trees leaf-felled in summer (cured for two weeks)	96	45
Spring wood seasoned for six months	98	30
Dry wood seasoned for 12 months and well-seasoned air-dry wood**	100	25

* At this level 15% of the energy is lost in the evaporation process.

** At this level 4% of the energy is lost in the evaporation process.

Source: U.S. Department of Energy, "Heating with Wood," Government Printing Office, Washington, D.C. May, 1980.

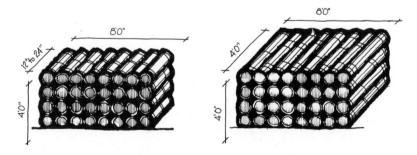

3-9. Face cord and full cord of wood. There is a difference.

Large deciduous trees can shade an area or structure from the hot summer sun while allowing the desired winter sunlight to pass through the bare branches (fig. 3-10). Dense evergreen trees, planted in well-located masses, can protect a structure from the unwanted chilling effect of winter winds (fig. 3-11). Even vegetation such as turf, vines, flower beds, and other ground covers will reduce the impact of unwanted summer heat when used instead of paved surfaces (fig. 3-12).

Shading of any type that protects paved surfaces is also effective in creating an overall cooler summertime environment. Since trees can in-

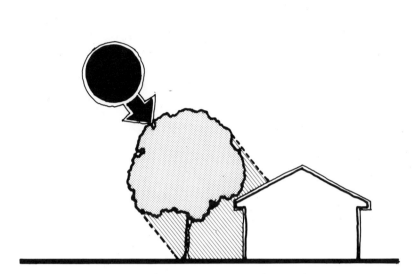

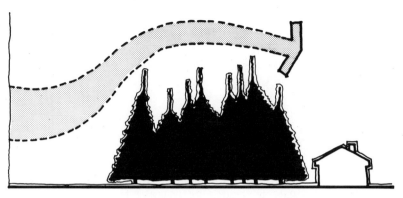

3-11. Large evergreen trees can be used to block, direct, or deflect winter winds.

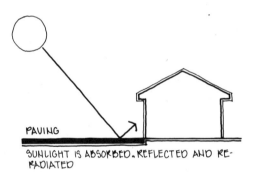

PAVING

SUNLIGHT IS ABSORBED, REFLECTED AND RE-RADIATED

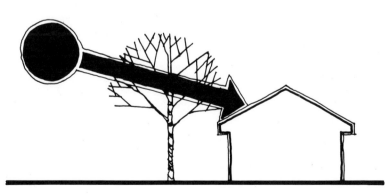

3-10. Large deciduous trees can shade a structure in the summer while allowing the sun to pass through in the winter. Limbs, branches, and twigs intercept 20 to 40 percent of the winter sun.

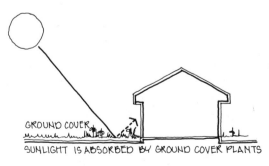

GROUND COVER

SUNLIGHT IS ABSORBED BY GROUND COVER PLANTS

3-12. Ground cover in place of paved surfaces will reduce reflected heat.

tercept and reflect, disperse, or absorb almost all the radiation that falls upon them, they can greatly reduce the amount of solar gain on the paved surfaces beneath them. The reflected heat from a paved surface combined with the released heat that is stored within it can add to the uncomfortable mean radiant temperature of an area (table 3–3). Shading can reduce this impact.

Table 3-3 Mean radiant temperature (MRT)
A person will feel comfortable (i.e., at 70°) with this air/surface temperature combination.

Air Temperature (in degrees F)	Average Surface Temperature (in degrees F)
49	85
56	80
63	75
70	70
77	65
84	60
91	55

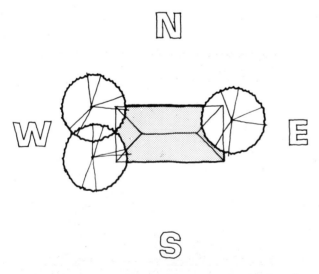

3-13. Deciduous overstory trees planted to the east and to the west of a structure can provide shade from the low morning and afternoon summer sun.

Trees can help cool a structure in the hot summer months. Deciduous trees installed to the east or west of the structure will prevent the branches from blocking the sun in the winter and be of greatest benefit in the summer. This arrangement will still provide some cooling. The branches will shade the east and west sun, and will overhang the building as they grow providing southern sun protection, since the sun is directly south only a small part of the day (fig. 3–13).

Shading from deciduous vegetation also closely follows the climatic seasons (fig. 3–14). At the spring equinox, for instance, most decid-

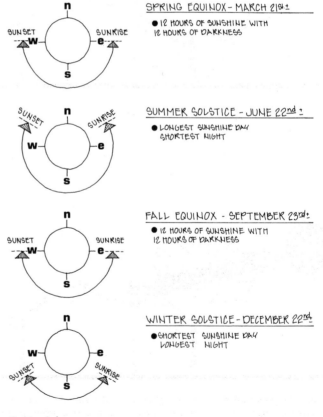

3-14. Solar seasons.

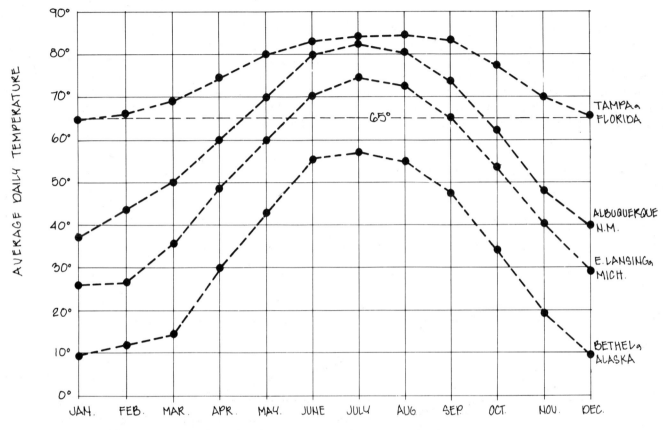

3-15. Average monthly temperatures for four selected cities in the United States. Note that the average July and August temperatures are generally warmer than the June temperatures.

uous trees are still bare so the desired spring sunlight will pass through them. At the fall equinox, however, the trees are still in full leaf and they effectively can block the undesired sun. The summer solstice is about June 22, but the hottest part of the summer usually occurs during July and August. This means that even though the sun is lower in the sky, the hottest weather of the season occurs after the middle of the solar summer. In September, when it is still warm and shading is still desirable, the leaves of the deciduous trees provide that shade (fig. 3-15).

Vegetation as a Sound Barrier

Plants are often promoted as effective barriers to unwanted sounds. Trees, shrubs, and ground-cover plants are installed along highways, next to industrial sites, near airports, and between other noise-producing activities and their neighbors. Although much debate continues about the overall effectiveness of vegetation alone, some documented studies show that dense plantings of trees and shrubs can be an effective means of sound attenuation.

These studies reveal that, along with the perceived benefit caused by the masking of the sound source from sight, actual noise reduction is achieved through the scattering and absorption of the sound waves by the vegetation (fig. 3–16). Solid masses of plant material, with vegetation continuous from the ground plain to the tops of the trees, are the most effective barriers (fig. 3–17). This is particularly true if evergreen trees are used along with small trees and shrubs beneath that fill any voids below the evergreen canopy. In addition, unwanted sounds can be masked by the "noise" created by the plants themselves. The rustling of leaves and the sound of the wind whistling through the needles of evergreens can hide some of the unwanted sounds (fig. 3–18).

Sound is typically measured in decibels. The A-weighted decibel, or dBA, is the measurement most commonly used. A change of one to two dBA is the lowest limit of change perceptible by the human ear (table 3–4).

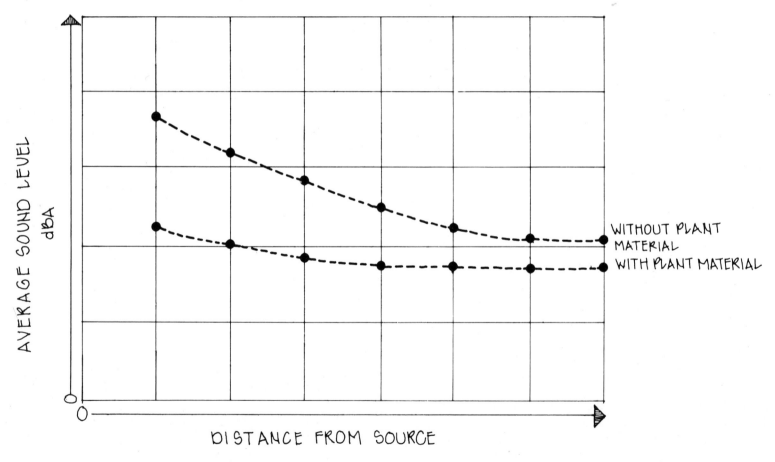

3–16. Noise-reducing ability of plant material.

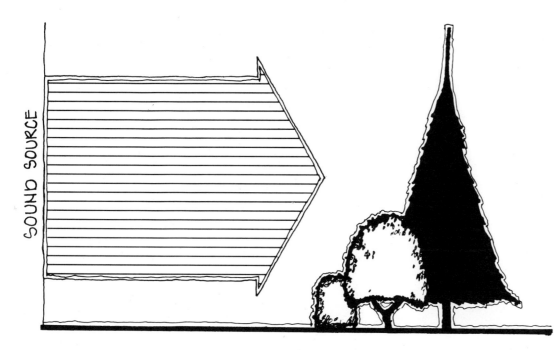

3-17. Solid masses of vegetation, with plants extending from the canopy down to the ground plain, can be an effective sound barrier.

3-18. The sound of the wind moving through the leaves and the movement of the leaves themselves can mask some external noise.

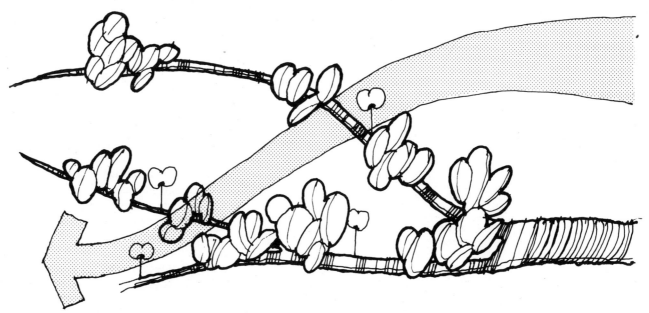

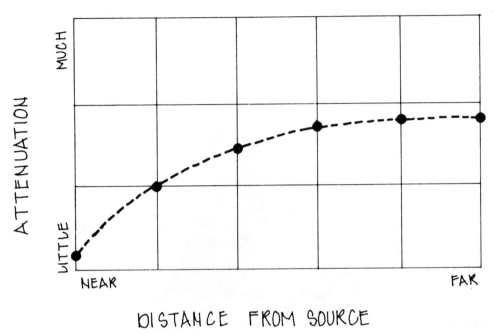

3-19. Relative sound attenuation of plant material.

Table 3-4 Typical noise levels in decibels of different activities

Decibels dBA	Activity
130	
120	Threshold of pain/injury
110	
100	Automobile horn
90	Heavy traffic/jackhammer
80	
70	
60	Busy street
50	Busy department store
40	Average office
30	
20	Whispers
10	Rustle of leaves

Excessive noise affects us physically, psychologically, and socially. Noise can damage hearing. Excessively loud music, factory noise, and even some traffic noise have all been shown to cause temporary and/or permanent hearing reduction. Noise can make people irritable, reduce their ability to perform tasks, increase stress, and cause other psychological problems. It can also interfere with normal conversation and reduce our ability to communicate.

Although studies on the effectiveness of vegetation as a sound barrier have shown that plants are effective (fig. 3-19), most have also shown that when plants are used in conjunction with land forms, the result is an immediately perceptible, permanent reduction in sound (fig. 3-20). The land form alone is more effective than the plant material alone, and the combination of the two reduces sound most effectively. It also creates an aesthetically pleasing buffer (fig. 3-21).

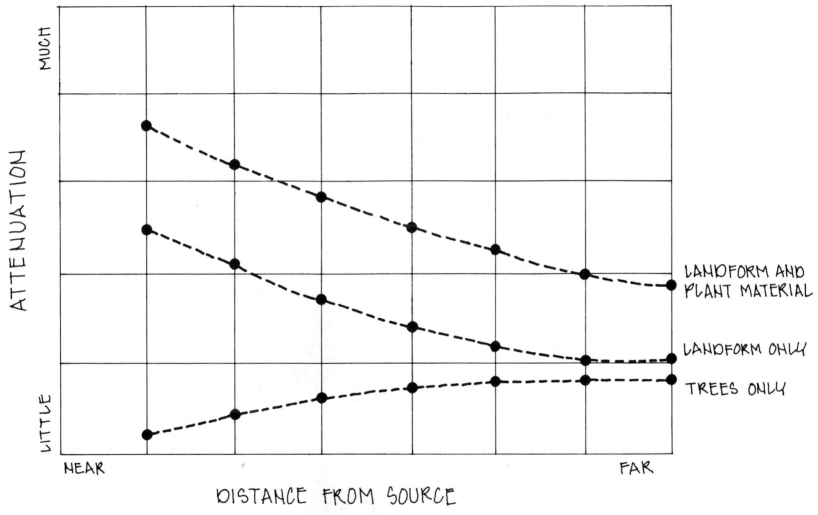

3-20. Sound attenuation based on distance from source with plant material alone, landform alone, and plant material and landform together.

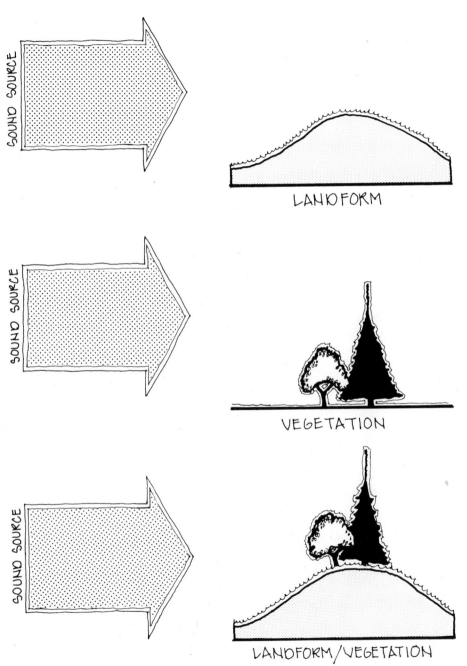

SOUND SOURCE

LANDFORM

SOUND SOURCE

VEGETATION

SOUND SOURCE

LANDFORM/VEGETATION

3-21. Sound attenuation is best achieved by the combination of vegetation and landforms.

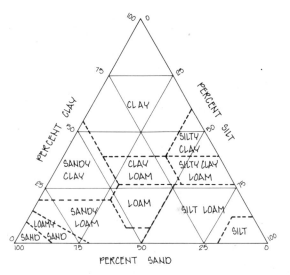

3–22. Feret Soil Classification System.

LAND

Land is commonly described as that part of the earth's surface above water. It is a medium for plant growth, the source for most of the physical materials we use, and a resource that man has extensively modified. He has drilled, mined, farmed, eroded, moved, compacted, polluted, paved over, built upon, worshipped, and cursed it. Today, man's very survival is dependent upon his ability to understand the basic characteristics of the land and the way that land uses affect those characteristics.

This section will attempt to identify some of the important land characteristics that directly influence the design of earth-sheltered structures and their landscapes. Specifically, there are three general categories: soil, slope, and orientation. Each of these will be discussed in relation to earth-sheltered landscapes.

Soil

"Soil" is the term used to describe the outermost layer of the earth's land. Its usage incorporates the rich farm land of the central United States, the red clays of the eastern states, the sands of the arid southwest, and even the rocky surface of the mountains in Colorado. Soil is a diverse collection of materials found on or near the earth's surface.

The basic materials of a soil are either organic matter, plants and animals, or inorganic matter, essentially mineral material derived from some "parent source," its original material. The organic matter can be living plants and creatures, or it can be the remains and residue of past life. The parent material can be as near as the underlying bedrock, broken down by the weathering process into soil-size particles. It may also have originated a great distance away, and the soil particles transported by various means to the present site. Soil material can be moved from one location to another by wind, water, glacial action, or other natural means. Of course, man has invented many ways of moving soil as well.

Classification The mineral-matter content of a given soil is often used to classify or categorize that soil. Specifically, soils are often defined according to the mixture of soil particle sizes. The Feret system separates soil particles into various groups, each with an accepted definition, which provides a universally understood method of classifying a particular soil (fig. 3–22).

Soil may be further defined or categorized by soil type or soil series. The soil-series classification describes certain qualities of a given soil. It also identifies the soil's profile, its composition from the upper surface through its entire depth. Soils have a natural tendency to form layers or horizons, and the soil-series categorization describes the thickness, arrangement, color, texture, mineral, organic-matter content, and other important characteristics of those layers.

Soil-series names literally number in the thousands. However, except for the possibility of different textures in the surface layer, soils with the same soil-series name have similar characteristics. The soil series name is typically a geographic name (lake, city, village, and the like) in the area where the soil was first located. These names provide another means of identifying soils in a universally understood manner.

Specific soil information for any particular site can usually be located in the publications of the local Soil Conservation Service. The service's address can be found in the phone book under United States Government, Department of Agriculture. A soil survey has usually been prepared on a county-wide basis providing information on drainage, erosion, depth to bedrock, depth to water table, mineral matter content, soil particle sizes, and soil series. Although the information is usually oriented to crop production or other agricultural activities, the maps, charts, graphs, and general documentation are all pertinent to earth-sheltered structures as well.

Soil Creation   The factors affecting the creation of a particular soil are generally as follows.

Parent material. The original source of the soil material, its parent material, may be nearby or far away and may be organic or mineral. It makes up the dominant content of the soil layer (fig. 3–23).

Vegetation. The organic covering over an existing soil has an effect

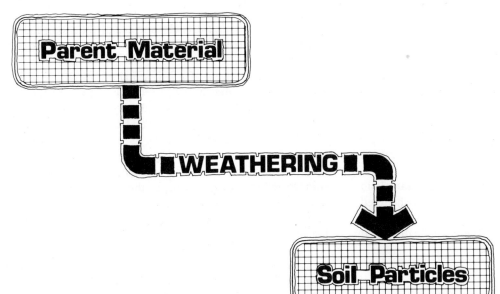

3–23. Different parent material will produce various types of soils.

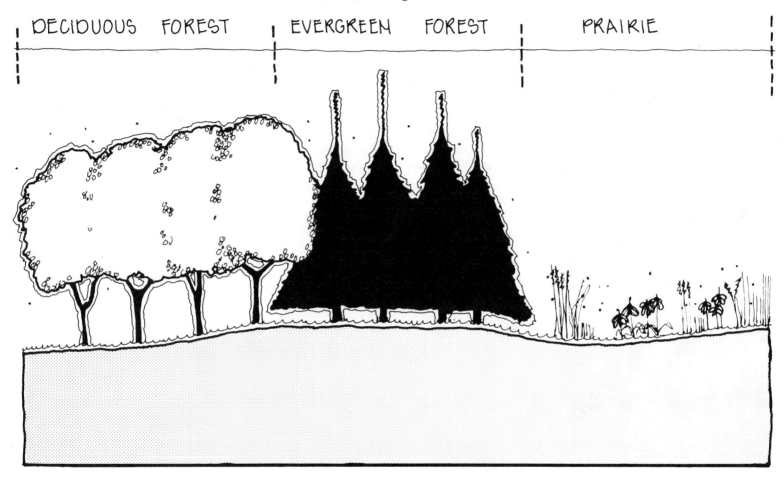

DECIDUOUS FOREST | EVERGREEN FOREST | PRAIRIE

3–24. Different plant covers will create different soils even though all other soil-creation factors are the same.

upon the makeup of the soil. Even with the same parent material, soils that develop under different types of vegetative cover will be of different soil-series. Various vegetative covers create differences in soil moisture content, organic matter content, erosion, soil organisms, and countless other factors, each of which will cause a slightly different soil series to result.

In the midwestern United States, for example, the prairie landscape that has existed for thousands of years created soils different from those found in tree-covered areas, even though the parent source of the two soils is the same (fig. 3–24). Where prairies, hardwood forests (birches, maples, and basswoods), and coniferous forests (spruces, firs, and pines) had similar parent material, the three different vegetative covers created three distinct soils.

The prairie soils were deep, black in color, and organically rich. The fibrous root systems of the prairie plants added tremendous amounts of organic matter to the soil. The extensiveness of the root systems pulled nutrients up to the surface from deep soil layers and from the underlying parent material.

The hardwood forest soils were somewhat similar in that they too tended to be nutrient-rich due to roots drawing up nutrients from deep in the soil. The organic layer was not as thick or extensive as that of the prairie soils, however, partially because the tree roots are not as concentrated as the roots of the prairie plants.

The nutrients in the soils created beneath coniferous forests tended to be leached out—that is, removed by the percolation of water down through the soil's upper layers and deposited at lower layers. The evergreen needles that litter the forest floor are low in basic nutrient salts but rich in organic and inorganic acids, making the topsoil somewhat acidic. Both prairie and hardwood forest soils on the other hand tend to be rich in bases such as calcium, deposited in the litter of the prairie plants and tree leaves respectively.

Coniferous soils tend to be distinctly layered, with individual layers or horizons often identifiable by stark color changes. Hardwood soils are usually not so distinctly layered. Prairie soils may seem homogeneous from the dark-colored surface down to the parent material. These color differences are all caused by the differing amounts of nutrients, water, organic matter, and so on found in each of the different soils, which in turn are based upon the vegetation that has grown in the parent material and created the soil.

Orientation. As the naturally occurring vegetation on a site helps determine the makeup of the soil, so does the orientation of a site help determine the type of vegetation. A south-facing slope, for instance, has a different type of naturally occurring vegetation than a north-facing slope in the same area. Each orientation tends to have certain predictable soil series associated with that orientation (fig. 3-25).

Where prairie and hardwood forest plant communities occur in the

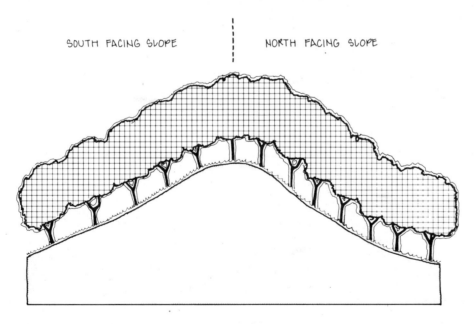

SOUTH FACING SLOPE   NORTH FACING SLOPE

3-25. The orientation of the land helps to determine the soil directly and indirectly. For instance, the orientation to the sun, winds, and other climatic influences will directly influence how a particular soil evolves. Indirectly, however, the orientation also helps to determine the vegetation of the site (adaptation), and the vegetative cover affects the soil formation.

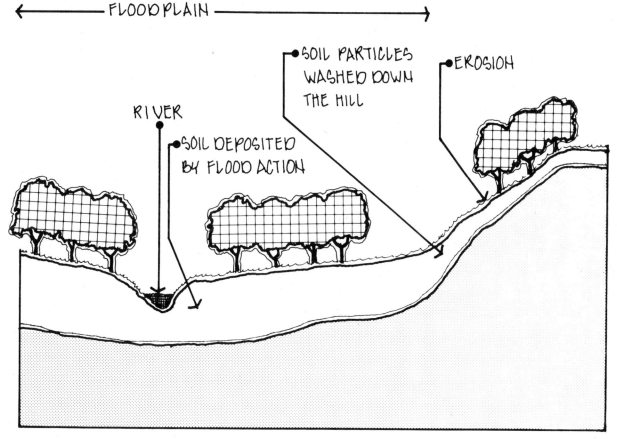

FLOOD PLAIN

SOIL PARTICLES WASHED DOWN THE HILL

EROSION

RIVER

SOIL DEPOSITED BY FLOOD ACTION

3-26. Moisture also affects soil creation. Wet areas, eroded areas, and dry exposed sites all have somewhat different soils. River valleys tend to have soils created by flood action and by the depositing of soil particles from the higher areas surrounding the flood plain.

same region, one factor that often determines whether a particular site will have prairie or hardwood forest species is the site's orientation. A south-facing slope in this region with its full, hot, dry sun, would more likely support a cover of prairie species. A cool, moist, partially shaded north-facing slope would more probably support forest species. The soils that develop beneath the prairie and forest vegetative covers of course are different, even if the parent material is the same.

Orientation may also help determine the general lay of the land. For instance, in an elongated mountain range, or sierra, south-facing slopes often tend to appear convex whereas north-facing slopes appear concave. This difference is primarily due to the large amounts of ice and snow that accumulate on the shaded, cooler north-facing slopes. As this stored moisture melts, extensive erosion occurs that over time will result in a scoured, eroded, and concave appearance.

Moisture. The amount of surface and subsurface moisture also helps to determine the soil types of any given site. Surface water may deposit or erode soil particles. It may also create certain habitats for particular groups of vegetation. Subsurface moisture additionally affects the soil by affecting the pH, organic matter, soil texture, and countless other important characteristics, each of which directly results in a change in the soil (fig. 3–26).

Climate. Climate plays an important role in determining soil type.

General or macro-climate conditions directly influence the type of vegetation, and microclimatic conditions may result in an isolated pocket of an uncommon soil within a generally homogenous site. The overall climate influences the type of vegetation found naturally at a site, and the vegetation helps to determine soil types. Climate also affects other determinants of soil types. Rainfall amounts, evaporation rates, and temperatures have a great affect on the eventual makeup of the soil. Moisture combined with freezing temperatures, for instance,

can help break down a rocky surface by fracturing the stone into smaller, soil-particle sizes (fig. 3–27).

Time. The creation of soil is not an overnight process. It is a geological phenomenom that occurs over time measured in decades and centuries. For example, it is estimated that the deep prairie soils of the midwestern United States were created at a rate of about one inch every one hundred years. The process of succession through time also changes the type of vegetation that exists, and the change in vegetative

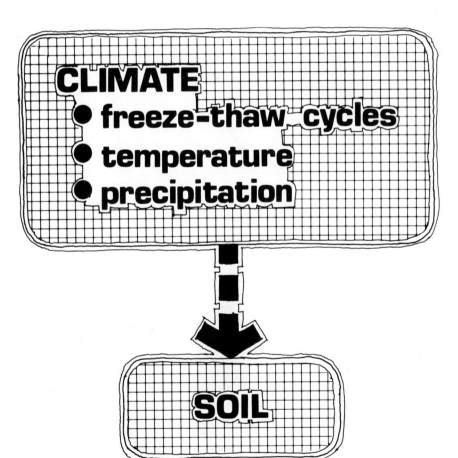

3–27. Climate influences soil creation directly through weathering action and indirectly by determining vegetative cover.

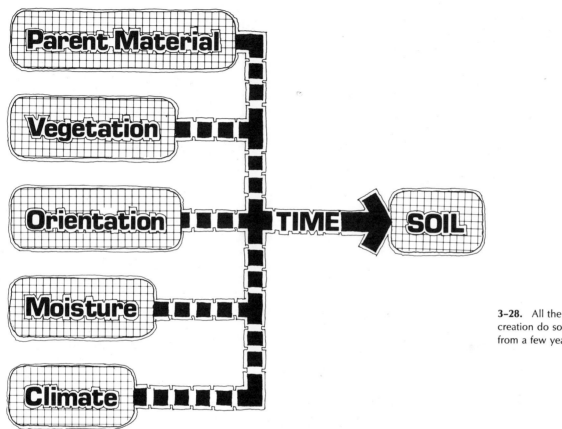

3–28. All the factors that influence soil creation do so over various lengths of time, from a few years to thousands of years.

cover of course changes the soil's makeup (fig. 3–28).

Temperatures   The normal soil temperature below the surface is about 55 degrees F. almost everywhere in the world. The surface temperature, however, is extremely wide-ranging, often reaching extremes beyond that of the surrounding air temperatures. The soil surface of a forest floor in the upper midwest, for instance, can reach a high of 120 to 130 degrees F. during the clear days of early spring, much higher than the outside air. Soil at twenty feet below the surface, however, has been shown to remain relatively constant throughout the year.

Temperature fluctuations in the soil on a day-to-day basis and from season to season are not as varied as might be thought, particularly as measured just a few feet below the surface (fig. 3–29). On a seasonal basis in the upper midwest, air-temperature extremes from minus 30 degrees F. in the winter to 100 degrees F. in the summer are found. At three feet of soil depth, the difference between the coldest and warmest soil temperatures is only about 35 degrees, ranging from 65 degrees F. at the warmest to 30 degrees F. at the coldest. At a depth of ten feet, the soil temperature may drop only 40 degrees F., whereas the warmest may reach only 60 degrees F., a difference of 20 degrees.

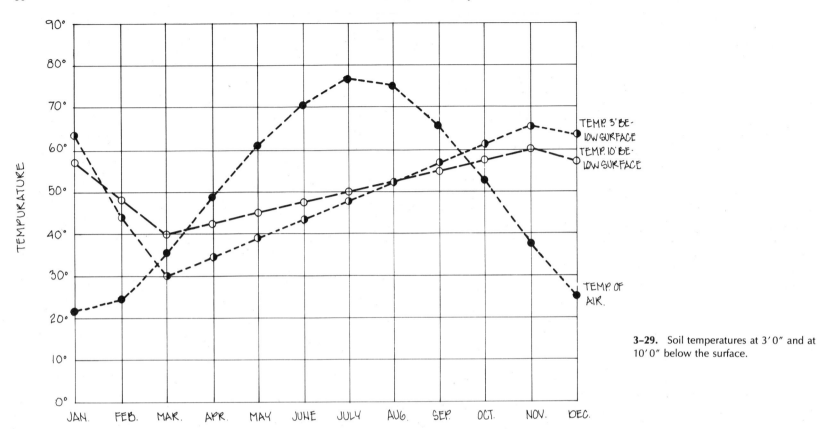

3-29. Soil temperatures at 3′ 0″ and at 10′ 0″ below the surface.

It is equally important to note that, although the soil temperature varies somewhat from season to season, the temperature changes occur very slowly and daily changes are very slight. At a depth of only one foot, the daily temperature change is almost imperceptible.

It has also been found that the highest and lowest seasonal temperatures are not necessarily found at the warmest and coldest air-temperature times of the year. The warmest soil recordings at certain depths come from the first part of November, whereas the coolest readings are found early in the spring. This means, of course, that the soils surrounding an earth-sheltered structure may be warmer than the air temperature late into the fall, helping to reduce the impact of

the cooling climate. In the early spring, when soil temperature may still be cool, the warmer outside air temperatures may be used to help keep the structures comfortable.

As mentioned previously, soil should not be used as insulation. Even when the late-fall soil is warmer than the outside air, it is still cooler than the desired internal air temperature. Thermal insulation is needed between the earth-sheltered structure and the surrounding soil. Although a soil covering will reduce the impact of the air temperature, it needs to be separated from the structure so that the soil does not act as a heat sink, which draws the internal warmth out to be dissipated into the soil.

Buffering   What a soil covering does accomplish, of course, is to separate the extremes of air temperatures from the surface of the structure by establishing a buffer between the two. Since the amount of heating or cooling needed is partially dependent upon the difference between the desired internal temperature and the external surface temperature, the less the difference in those temperatures, the less heating or cooling energy is necessary. Simply stated, if the temperature at the structure's external surface is close to the desired internal temperature, the amount of energy needed to raise or lower the internal temperature to the desired level will be minimized (fig. 3–30).

The soil covering also reduces rapid air movement's impact by creating a buffer between the wind and the structure. This reduces the problem of air infiltration. Cold winter air infiltrating into a structure is one of the major causes of discomfort for the occupants. The air can seep in through a seemingly solid wall, but the fact is walls have many tiny openings. Whether the openings are created for utilities, such as electrical outlets, or for structural reasons, gaps are almost always to be expected. An earth covering on a roof or wall prevents the infiltration by making it impossible for the wind to reach the surface of the structure.

Structure   As stated previously, soil is made up of particles of various sizes, materials, and mixtures. Soil is not, however, a solid

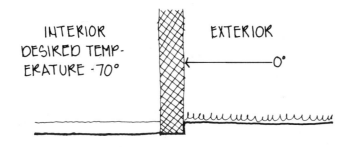

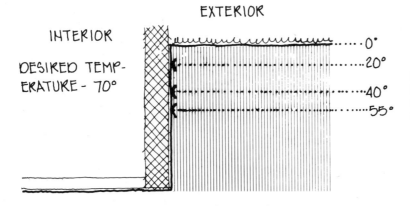

3–30. Keeping the interior at a desired temperature is made easier the closer the exterior temperature is to the desired interior temperature.

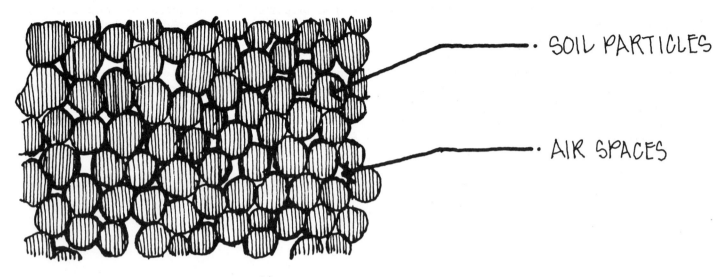

3-31. Soil contains voids or air spaces between particles.

mass of particles. It also contains voids or air spaces that allow air, water, nutrients, and other soil components to circulate. The voids are critical to the soil's proper functioning and to its quality, as well as the key to the movement of various items in the soil. Ideal soil composition would be made up of about 50 percent soil material (mineral and organic matter) and 50 percent air space (fig. 3–31). Air in the soil should be the same composition as air in the atmosphere. Poorly structured soil contains an excess of carbon dioxide and a lack of oxygen.

Ideal soil structure and composition, however, is seldom found in man-made landscapes. Earth moving, no matter how carefully accomplished, results in a soil with greatly reduced amounts of air spaces. This condition is usually referred to as *compaction,* or a loss of soil structure. Both pedestrian and vehicular traffic passing over the soil further increases compaction.

Compaction has a detrimental affect on the soil and on the plants that grow in the soil. Compaction results in many changes.

Compaction Reduces	Compaction Increases
Moisture availability	Runoff
Moisture absorption	Erosion
Oxygen content	Carbon dioxide content
Pore space	Thermal conductivity
Nutrient availability	Plant energy needed for root penetration

An anthropic soil mix (a mix produced from natural materials by the action of man) has been suggested to help remedy compacted-soil problems. It is explained in the following section.

Structure Improvement   To prevent potential plant and soil problems in earth-sheltered landscapes or in any other constructed landscape, and to minimize the problems inherent in compacted soils, adequate soil structure must be established. This may require that additives be incorporated into the soil to ensure proper texture, drainage, and structure (fig. 3–32). The improved soil will enhance the health and vigor of the plant material around the earth-sheltered structure.

Some basic soil additives and what they accomplish include the following.

Drainage material. To ensure that adequate pore spaces exist for moisture to drain out of the soil, a coarse-textured material can be added. Typically, this material is sand or very fine gravel, thoroughly mixed in with the existing soil.

Water retention. Although drainage material has been added to ensure proper moisture percolation, some means of retaining moisture in the root zone may also be necessary to make sure that not all the moisture drains out. An absorbent material that can retain water and make it available to plant roots should be added. Peat moss will function this way and will also add nutrients and a better overall texture to the soil. Incorporating it in the soil mix is beneficial both to the soil and its plants.

Weight lighteners. Since the soil mix may be placed upon the roof of an earth-sheltered structure, it is prudent to find a means of minimizing its dead-load weight. Soils can be extremely heavy, and some artificial materials may have to be incorporated into the soil mix to lessen the weight. Even though the structure is constructed to safe engineering standards, a lightweight soil mix will further lessen potential load problems. This is particularly important in retrofit situations, where existing structures are modified for rooftop planters or other general additions of planting areas.

An ideal material would be one that occupied space but added little weight itself. It would, as a side benefit, add texture and pore space to the soil. If the soil mix could also provide nutrients, so much the better, but it is not a requirement.

Small styrofoam beads are a commonly used material. Packaged under various brand names, they are usually less than a sixteenth or thirty-second of an inch in diameter. These beads have little weight themselves since they are composed mostly of air, and they can be incorporated easily into the soil mix.

Additional additives. Even with the addition of drainage and water-retention materials, the proper regulation of moisture in the soil mix may still be difficult. Periodic watering can aid overdrained soils, but an excessively, continuously wet soil presents other problems. A drainage tile system installed before the soil is added should help prevent these problems. Charcoal incorporated into the soil as well will

Existing Soil
+ drainage material
+ water retention material
+ lightweight material
+ additional additives

= SOIL MIX
(Good Quality & Texture)

3–32. Good soil texture can sometimes be achieved only by adding certain materials to an existing soil.

help prevent excess moisture from "souring" the soil.

Plant nutrients will have to be added to the soil periodically to ensure continued plant health and vigor. Nutrients are continually being used up by the plants and are also leached out by the soil's natural drainage system. The exact quantities and mixtures of needed nutrients depend on many factors. Individual soil-nutrient needs can be determined by conducting soil tests through testing companies, county extension agencies, other private and governmental agencies, or by using soil-testing kits available from local garden-supply stores.

Slope

"Slope" is defined as the land's inclination or direction and degree of its rise or fall. It is typically described by a measurement based on the amount of elevation change, sometimes using descriptive but undefinitive terms such as "steep," "hazardous," "shallow," "flat," "precipitous," "sheer," "gentle," "moderate," and so on. The problem with these descriptions is that they are imprecise and their meanings may change from place to place. For instance, a Kansas wheat farmer's "steep slope" may be the same as a Colorado skier's "flat slope."

The more precise system quantifies the amount of slope by using more universally agreed-upon means of describing the change in elevation. Three methods are most commonly used to describe elevation change accurately: percentage, ratio, or measurement of angle (fig. 3–33).

Percentage   The *percentage* method of describing the amount of slope is one of the most common. The percentage figure represents the amount of change in vertical elevation that occurs over a certain horizontal distance. As an example, a 5-percent slope represents five feet of vertical change over a horizontal distance of one hundred feet:

VERTICAL DISTANCE ÷ HORIZONTAL DISTANCE = PERCENT SLOPE
(5 feet)   +   (100 feet)   =   (0.05) or (5%)

Ratio   In the *ratio* method, the slope is described as the ratio between the horizontal distance (always written first) and the vertical elevation change (usually expressed as the number "1"). Again, using

five feet of elevation change and one hundred feet of horizontal distance, the ratio would be 20:1:

HORIZONTAL DISTANCE : VERTICAL DISTANCE
(100 feet)   :   (5 feet)
(Simplified)   20 : 1

Angle   The *angle* method is not as commonly used as the first two. Once again, using five feet and one hundred feet, the slope would be two degrees and fifty-two minutes (approximately). This is determined by using a trigonometric formula to find the tangent of the angle formed by the vertical change from the horizontal.

TANGENT = VERTICAL DISTANCE ÷ HORIZONTAL DISTANCE
TANGENT =   (5 feet)   ÷   (100 feet)
TANGENT = 0.05
    ANGLE = 2°52′ ± (from trigonometric tables)

See table 3–5 for a comparison of the three methods.

Table 3–5   Slopes expressed as percentage, ratio, and as angle

Vertical Change (100′ Horizontal Length)	Percent Slope	Ratio	Angle of Slope (Approximate)
1′	1	100:1	0° 34′
2′	2	50:1	1° 09′
5′	5	20:1	2° 52′
10′	10	10:1	5° 43′
20′	20	5:1	11° 19′
25′	25	4:1	14° 02′
33$\frac{1}{3}$′	33$\frac{1}{3}$	3:1	18° 26′
50′	50	2:1	26° 34′
100′	100	1:1	45° 00′
200′	200	1:2	63° 26′

Orientation

"Orientation" can be defined as the direction that a given object faces. The direction of a slope, its orientation, is as important to earth-sheltered landscapes as its amount. Understanding the complex relationships between the orientation of the land and the wind and sun is a

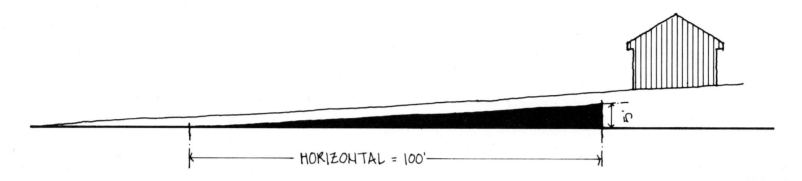

●PERCENTAGE METHOD = $\dfrac{\text{VERTICAL DISTANCE}}{\text{HORIZONTAL DISTANCE}} = \dfrac{5'}{100'} = 0.05$ OR 5%

●RATIO METHOD = HORIZONTAL DISTANCE : VERTICAL DISTANCE = 100:5 OR 20:1

●ANGLE METHOD = TAN = $\dfrac{\text{VERTICAL DISTANCE}}{\text{HORIZONTAL DISTANCE}} = \dfrac{5}{100} = 0.05$ OR 2°52'*

*FROM TANGENT TABLES

3-33. Slope calculated by percentage, ratio, and angle methods.

key to the goals of reducing foreign energy dependency and increasing energy independence.

In order to comprehend the importance of orientation, it is necessary first to have a clear understanding of what a specifically described orientation means. For instance, a wall that faces south has a south orientation. The orientation of a section of pitched roof that slopes downward to the north is north. The windows on the east side of a structure have an east orientation. A piece of land that slopes from east to west—that is, the land is higher in elevation in the east and lower in the west—has a west orientation (fig. 3–34).

The importance of understanding how an object's orientation influences the energy decisions made is shown by the following analysis.

In much of the northern United States, the south wall of a structure will receive as much solar radiation in the winter months as it will in the summer. The lower winter sun angle shines on a vertical wall more efficiently from a solar radiation standpoint than the higher sun angles of summer, and this fact, if taken advantage of in the building of the structure, also increases the amount of radiation. The inclusion of properly sized sun screens, overhangs, and correctly selected and placed vegetation will reduce the amount of summer radiation received. East and west walls of a structure receive two and one-half times more solar radiation in the summer than they do in the winter. The summer radiation from the east and west is low-angled and usually undesired, since excess warming is not wanted in the summer. Therefore, to maximize the total solar gain in the winter and to minimize the solar gain in the summer, the optimum orientation for a structure is south, with the long axis of the structure east to west. Glass areas likewise should be maximized on the south and minimized everywhere else (fig. 3–35).

The land's orientation is tied directly to the energy-efficiency possibilities of a structure. Typically, a south-oriented slope would be considered the optimum site for construction of an energy-efficient structure. Despite this fact, even east, west, north, and flat sites can, through design and land manipulation, all be effective as earth-sheltered sites.

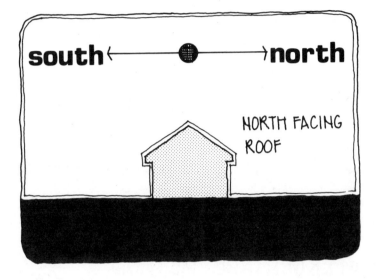

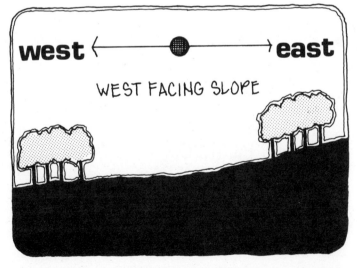

3–34. Orientation can be defined as the direction that a given object faces.

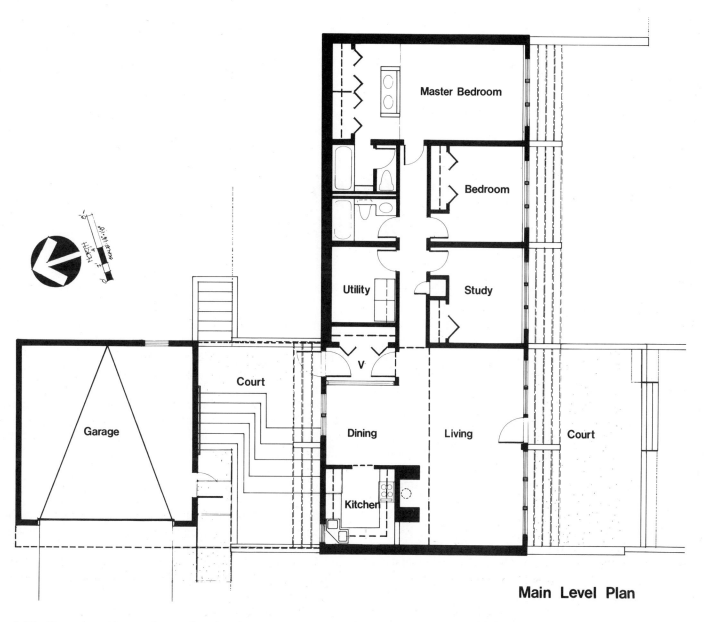

Master Bedroom

Bedroom

Utility

Study

Court

Garage

Dining

Living

Court

Kitchen

V

Main Level Plan

3–35. The structure does not have to face directly south, but the glass area should be oriented within 30 degrees of south to maximize solar effectiveness. (Drawing courtesy Green Meadows Ltd.)

4

Natural Elements II: Sun and Wind

THE SUN is the ultimate source of almost all our energy. (Nuclear, geothermal, and tidal energy are not solar-based, although the sun does contribute somewhat to tidal action.) It is the source of the energy that is captured, converted, and stored by green plants. The sun is the main generator of wind, either directly or indirectly, and it is the ultimate energy source for hydroelectric power generation by way of the water cycle (fig. 4–1). Solar energy is clean, free, and available worldwide. No one owns it or controls it and therefore no one can influence its distribution or charge for its use. It is the only energy source that is delivered to your home, factory, office, or farm every day of the year at no cost to you. It is the equal-opportunity energy source.

How Much Energy?

The average temperature of the sun's interior is estimated at over 23 million degrees F. (13 million degrees C.). The surface, meanwhile, is estimated to be "only" 10,000 degrees F. (5,500 degrees C.). While only one five-billionth (1/5,000,000,000) of the energy from the sun hits the earth's atmosphere, that amount is still enough to keep our planet alive and to supply most of our direct energy needs.

The total solar energy that strikes the earth per day is equivalent to the energy in 684 billion tons of coal. On a clear day, each square meter of the earth's surface receives an average of 15,000 calories per minute or some 9 million calories per ten-hour day. In Btus that means an average of 1500 Btus per square foot per day.

All the averages must be balanced with the fact that certain geographical areas receive different amounts of energy (sunlight) depending on the season and the climatic conditions that exist at any one time. Still, the energy available is tremendous and remains today a largely untapped resource.

Sun Angles

Information typically found in almost all the solar reference books concerns the various sun angles applicable to solar design. The earth-sheltered-landscape designer needs to be aware of two angles to evaluate a site accurately and to plan structure location, orientation, and "south face" exposure in order to maximize winter sun and minimize summer sun.

The first angle is the sun's *azimuth* (fig. 4–2). The azimuth is the angle of the sun, measured in a horizontal plane, from some established direction (usually north).

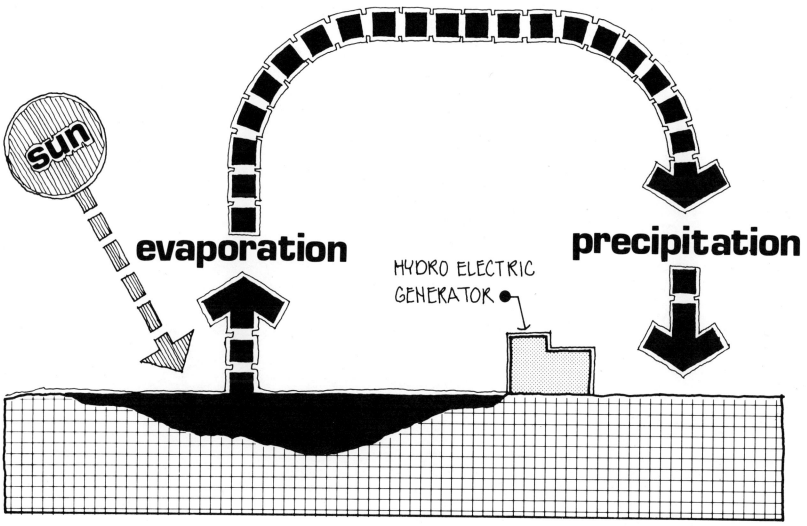

4–1. Solar energy powers the water cycle.

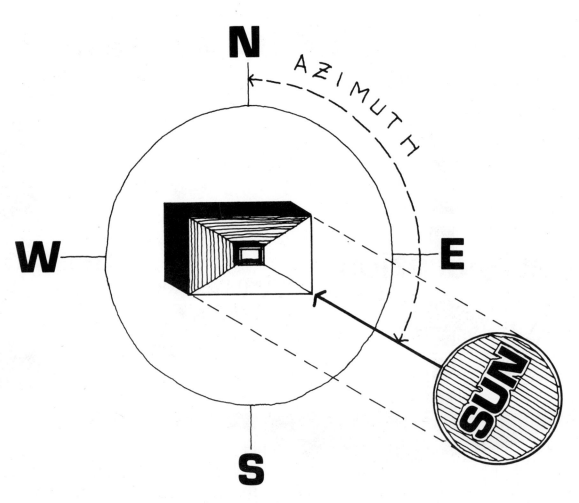

4–2. The *azimuth* is the sun's position relative to direct north.

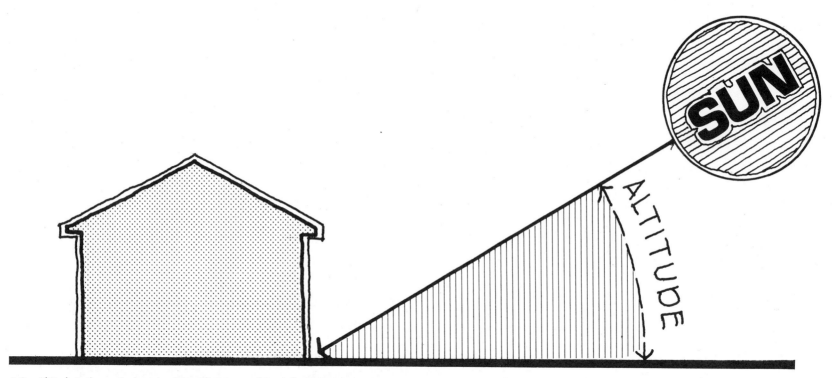

4–3. *Altitude* is the vertical angle of the sun measured from the horizon.

The second angle is the *altitude* of the sun (fig. 4–3). The altitude is the vertical angle of the sun measured from the horizon. At sunrise and sunset, the altitude or angle of the sun is 0° since the sun is at the horizon. It reaches its highest altitude of the day at solar noon, when the sun is directly south (180° from true north).

Both the azimuth and the altitude vary over the four seasons. They both reach their maximums and minimums on the summer and winter solstices (table 4–1). Reference books can supply detailed information, charts, and graphs on exact solar angles for every minute of every day of the year for almost any location in the world (fig. 4–4). It is important here simply to know where the sun rises and sets, what the relative azimuths and altitudes are for various times of the year, and that the

4-4. Latitudes across the United States.

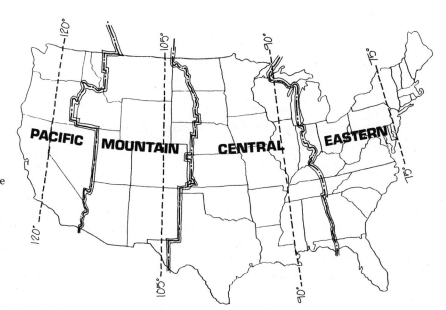

4-5. Time zones. Only in the approximate center of a time zone does solar noon equal clock noon, and that occurs only when the clock is set to Standard Time.

daily solar sweep (the movement of the sun from east to west during the course of a day) averages about 15 degrees of movement (azimuth) per hour.

Table 4-1 Seasonal Variations in Azimuth and Altitude

Latitude	Season	Sunrise Sunset Azimuth	Sunrise Time	Sunset Time	Day Length	Solar Noon Altitude
50	Winter	128 30′	8:00	4:00	8 hr.	16 30′
	Fall/Spring	90	6:00	6:00	12 hr.	40
	Summer	51 30′	4:00	8:00	16 hr.	63 30′
45	Winter	124 30′	7:40	4:20	8 hr. 40 min.	21 30′
	Fall/Spring	90	6:00	6:00	12 hr.	45
	Summer	55 30′	4:20	7:40	15 hr. 20 min.	68 30′
40	Winter	121	7:30	4:30	9 hr.	26 30′
	Fall/Spring	90	6:00	6:00	12 hr.	50
	Summer	59	4:30	7:30	15 hr.	73 30′
35	Winter	119	7:10	4:50	9 hr. 40 min.	31 30′
	Fall/Spring	90	6:00	6:00	12 hr.	55
	Summer	61 30′	4:50	7:10	14 hr. 20 min.	78 30′
30	Winter	117 30′	7:00	5:00	10 hr.	36 30′
	Fall/Spring	90	6:00	6:00	12 hr.	60
	Summer	62 30′	5:00	7:00	14 hr.	83 30′
25	Winter	116 30′	6:50	5:10	10 hr. 20 min.	41 30′
	Fall/Spring	90	6:00	6:00	12 hr.	65
	Summer	88 30′	5:10	6:50	13 hr. 40 min.	88 30

NOTES:
1. All times shown are Standard Time.
2. Sunrise and sunset are 12 hours apart and the solar azimuth is 90 degrees on the fall and spring equinox dates.
3. Noon azimuth is always 180 degrees, directly south, at solar noon.
4. Sunrise and sunset altitudes are 0 degrees.

It should also be clarified that solar noon is the middle of the sun's day and is not necessarily the noon on our clocks. Solar noon always occurs when the sun is directly south and is at its highest altitude of the day. Solar noon and clock noon would correspond only at the approximate center of the time zone and only when the clock was set on Standard Time (fig. 4–5). The closer to the edge of a particular time zone, the less directly south the sun will be at clock noon (fig. 4–6). At the western edge of a particular time zone, solar noon will occur after clock noon. At the eastern edge of that zone, however, solar noon—when the sun is at its highest daily altitude and is directly south—will occur before clock noon (fig. 4–7).

The use of Daylight Savings Time affects the time shown on the clock but in no way affects when solar noon occurs. Daylight Savings Time noon is one hour different from Standard Time noon, and DST's relationship to solar noon is one hour different as well. Solar noon corresponds to 11:00 DST, which moves the clock setting *back* one hour, but only in the approximate center of a given time zone. The eastern and western edges of the time zone would vary in the same way that they do in Standard Time.

Degree Days

Heating Degree Day or Degree Day (DD) is the measurement commonly used across the United States to determine energy needs. It is a measurement of the difference between the average daily temperature and the base temperature of 65 degrees F. (65 degrees F. is the exterior temperature at which no supplemental interior heat is needed to maintain comfort within a structure.) For example, if the average temperature for a day is 20 degrees F., then the Degree Day reading for that day would be 65 minus 20, or 45 DD. Average daily temperatures over 65 degrees F. would result in a 0 DD number and would indicate that there was no supplemental interior heat needed that day.

The individual Degree Day numbers are collected and a yearly summary is calculated. These yearly DD numbers are a relative indication of one location's heating needs compared to another's. The higher the DD number, the more supplemental heat that is necessary to maintain adequate interior temperatures, assuming all other circumstances, such as wind, orientation, and insulation are the same. For instance, Indianapolis, Indiana, with 5,600 DD, has less heating needs than does Madison, Wisconsin, at 7,700 DD, but more heating needs than Louisville, Kentucky, at 4,600 DD (fig. 4–8).

In the contiguous forty-eight states, the range in DD is from less than 100 DD at the southern tip of Florida to over 10,000 DD in northern Minnesota, northern North Dakota, and a few other isolated and scattered mountainous areas. Parts of Alaska are not much colder, with

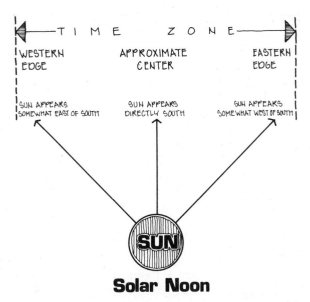

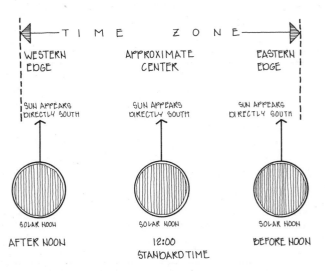

4-6. Depending on the location of the observer, the sun appears somewhat west, directly south, or somewhat east at clock noon (Standard Time) throughout the time zone.

4-7. The sun appears directly south only at the center of a time zone at noon, Standard Time.

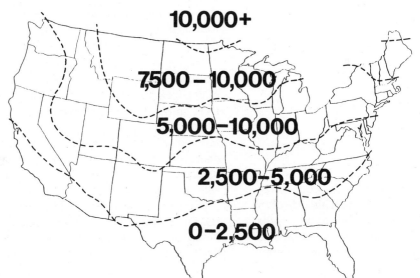

4-8. Degree Days across the United States.

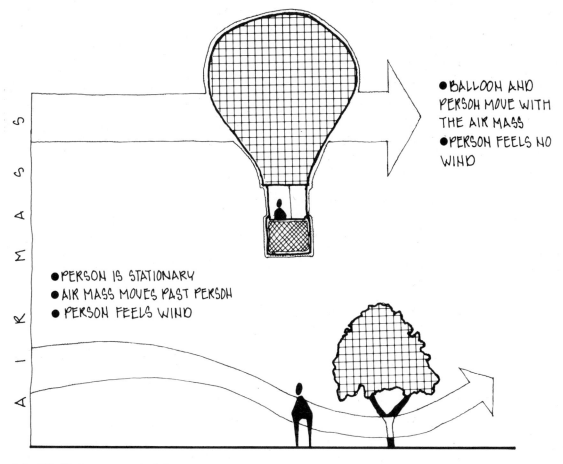

4-9. Wind is the movement of air masses.

Anchorage listed at just under 11,000 DD, but other Alaskan cities have Degree Day figures of 14,000 and above.

Exact Degree Day figures are available for almost any location. It should be remembered that the numbers are averages calculated over many years and that any particular year may have more or less heating requirements than indicated by the Degree Day figures. DD numbers are often broken down by months for various locations, and these too are averages and should be treated as such.

WIND

Wind is another important environmental factor that must be addressed when planning the earth-sheltered landscape. Wind is simply the movement of air generated by temperature differences between air masses. The air-temperature differences are caused directly by unequal solar heating or indirectly by the effect of solar-heated land masses and water bodies (fig. 4-9). Wind affects people directly in the exterior environment and indirectly through its effect on structures.

Comfort is affected by the wind through the force of the wind itself. Excessive wind force makes certain outdoor tasks impossible to perform and can make being outdoors unpleasant. Secondly, excessive winds can make normally acceptable temperatures uncomfortable, and if combined with cold temperatures, winds can be dangerous. The lack of wind can at times be equally uncomfortable. Thirdly, the amount of particulate matter moved about by the wind, whether small material such as dust and pollen or large material such as paper or other solid objects, can add to the discomfort in an outdoor situation.

Winds indirectly affect people in interior environments by directly influencing the structure. It has already been stated that winds can cool the interior of structures in the winter through infiltration and conduction (see fig. 2-4). Winds create areas of high pressure on the windward side of a structure, forcing air into the structure through the various gaps and cracks that occur on most buildings. Likewise, on the leeward side, the wind shadow creates an area of low pressure that causes interior air to be pulled out of the structure (fig. 4-10).

Much has been written about wind control, and various studies have documented the best methods of blocking or mitigating the impact of undesired cold winter winds (fig. 4-11). Additionally, many methods of encouraging, channeling, or directing summer breezes to achieve the desired temperature have been established. To control the wind's influences effectively, we must be aware of where winds come from at various times of the year, what their different effects are, how to control winds to best meet our needs, and how they might be used for energy savings.

Wind Data

To control and use the wind effectively, a designer must first know its direction, speed, and intensity during different times of the year. General wind data can be found in many reference books. It is available in depth from the National Climatic Center in Asheville, North Carolina. Local weather bureaus will have extensive data on area wind

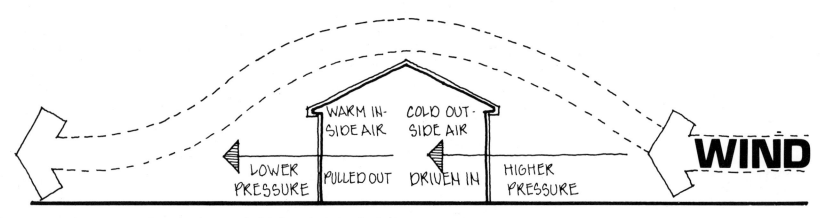

4-10. Winds create unequal pressures between the interior and exterior of a structure.

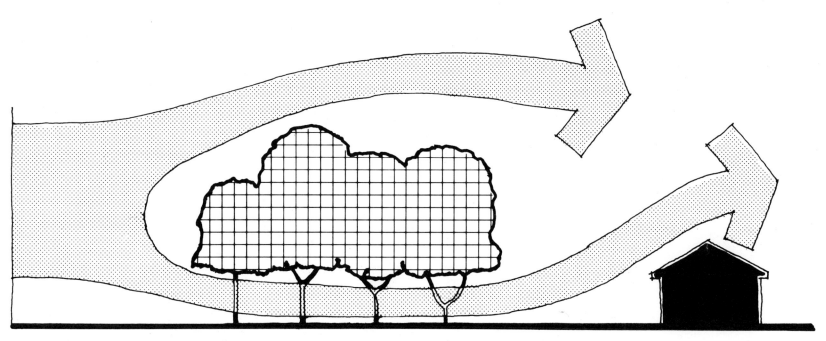

4-11. Some wind penetration in a wind break reduces the typical problem of snow deposits at the leeward side of the break.

conditions, as well as information on temperatures, degree days, precipitation, cloud cover, sunshine, and visibility. Such data is quite comprehensive and, although probably more detailed than necessary for our use, it can confirm or quantify the general information found in other references.

For instance, winds in Des Moines, Iowa, might be generalized as follows: southern breezes in the spring and summer and northerly winds in the fall and winter (fig. 4–12). Data from the National Oceanic and Atmospheric Administration (NOAA), National Weather Service Forecast Office at the Des Moines Municipal Airport, reveals that those generalizations, although accurate, reflect only part of the story. As figure 4–13 shows, wind direction can be stated generally but

must also be qualified with the knowledge that, like all natural systems, direction can be variable.

Trends can be predicted but wind can come from almost any direction during any season. As planners, we must use the data as well as we can to our advantage. Since we cannot block all the unwanted winds in the winter while at the same time encouraging the cooling breezes of summer, we need to find some reasonable compromise. That compromise is the well-established practice of creating a break or buffer on the north, west, and northwest sides of a structure to block the predominant winter winds. This wind break, combined with wind-encouraging openings set to the south of the structure, allows the impact of the wind to be controlled. (fig. 4–14).

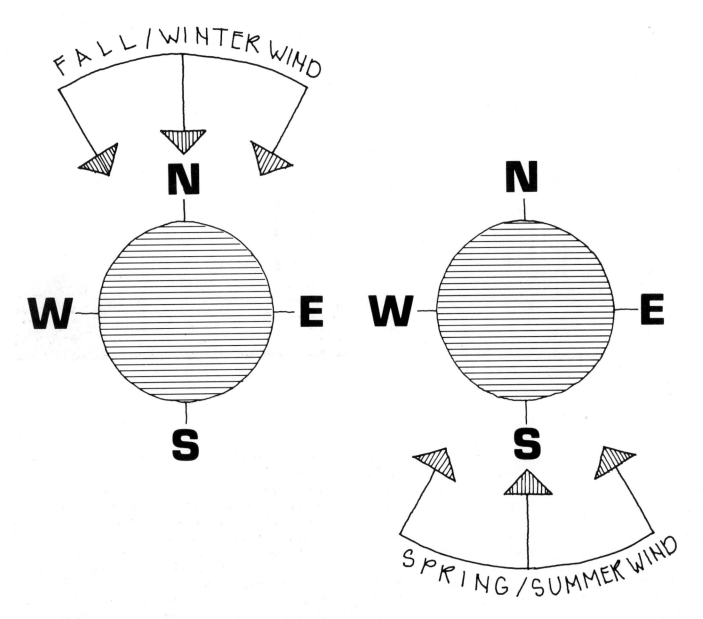

4-12. General wind patterns.

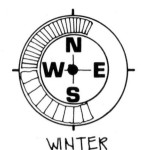

WINTER

- NOV., DEC., JAN., FEB., MARCH
- 51% OF WINTER WINDS COME FROM WEST, N.W. AND NORTH
- 24% OF WINTER WINDS FROM SOUTH AND SOUTHWEST

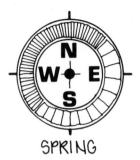

SPRING

- APRIL, MAY
- 40% OF THE SPRING WINDS COME FROM THE WEST, NORTH-WEST AND NORTH.
- 45% OF THE SPRING WINDS COME FROM EAST, S.E., AND SOUTH

SUMMER

- JUNE, JULY, AUGUST
- 49% OF THE SUMMER WINDS COME FROM THE SOUTH AND SOUTHWEST.
- 21% OF THE SUMMER WINDS COME FROM THE EAST AND SOUTHEAST

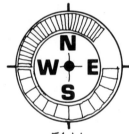

FALL

- SEPTEMBER, OCTOBER
- 50% OF THE FALL WINDS COME FROM THE SOUTHEAST, SOUTH. AND SOUTHWEST.
- 29% OF THE FALL WINDS COME FROM THE NORTH AND NORTHWEST

4-13. Wind direction by season. Compiled by Susan Erickson, Ames, Iowa, using ten years (1970–1980) of wind direction information as documented by the National Oceanic and Atmospheric Administration—National Weather Service Forecast Office, Municipal Airport, Des Moines, Iowa.

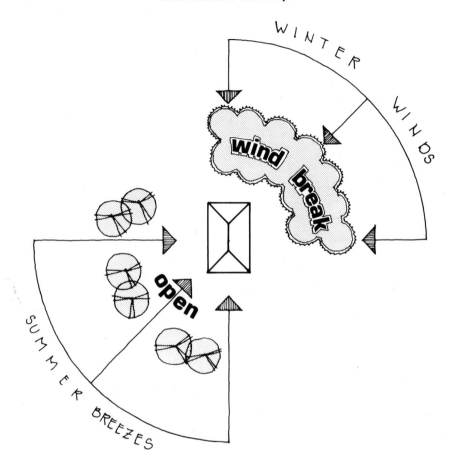

4-14. Schematic wind break and openings to block and encourage wind, respectively.

Wind Chill

One of the best-known effects of wind concerns the *wind-chill* factor, usually given as part of the weather forecast from late fall to spring in all cold-weather climates. The wind-chill factor is basically a measure of how much the wind increases the chilling effect of cool temperatures (see table 4–2). At air temperatures below 100 degrees F., air movement across skin creates a cooling sensation through convec-

tion and the evaporation of perspiration. Wind moving cool air over the skin's surface cools skin more than the cool air alone. Even winds as light as 15mph can reduce apparent temperatures by 20 to 30 degrees F.

Hypothermia, the reduction of body temperature, is a health hazard caused by the body losing heat faster than it can produce heat. Although it can happen to anyone, older people are particularly susceptible to hypothermia because of reduced or restricted blood circulation. Even at air temperatures near 70 degrees F., hypothermia is possible, especially with wet or windy conditions (see table 4–3).

Cold winds blowing on exposed skin can also cause frostbite, which is the actual freezing of skin tissue. It usually occurs with the fingers, toes, ears, and nose, although any tissue can be affected. Frostbite causes a loss of sensation and the skin may turn white or very pale. It can lead to serious consequences, including loss of the affected tissue or even death.

Wind as an Energy Source

The wind has been a source of energy that man has used for thousands of years to ease his labors. It has provided the energy to move ships, to turn wheels for grinding grain, to pump water out of the ground. However, in the twentieth century the use of wind power all but disappeared for several reasons: the advent of cheap and plentiful fossil fuels, the ever-increasing demand for energy, and the relative undependability of the wind (not always available in the proper quantity when needed).

Today, wind is once again being looked upon as a possible alternative energy source. New technology has vastly increased the efficiency of the old-fashioned windmill, and a new generation of wind-driven generators is available. The new generators convert the rotating action of the blades (which are set either on a vertical or horizontal axis) to the production of electricity (fig. 4–15). The output can be either direct current (DC), which can be stored in batteries for later use

when the wind is not sufficient to provide electricity, or alternating current (AC), which can be tied into the structure's electrical system through a simple switching device. The latter has become a standard procedure due to the federal requirement that local utility companies must purchase back any excess power generated by a customer if the customer both generates electricity and uses the utility power as a backup source. This means that when the wind generator is working most efficiently and is creating more electricity than the structure needs, the excess is put into the utility company's line and is registered at the meter box as a credit to the customer. Under ideal circumstances, sufficient winds would exist to operate an efficient wind-driven generator, which would result in no electricity having to be purchased from the utility company.

Unfortunately, given the cost of today's systems (averaging about $2,000 per kilowatt), the energy costs saved usually cannot justify the costs of a system. Since it generally takes a two-kilowatt system to run basic household appliances and a ten-kilowatt system to include the heating and cooling systems in a house, installing a wind generator is not a decision to be made lightly. Four problems must be addressed.

Average Wind Speed It is generally acknowledged that it takes an average wind speed of 10mph or more for a wind-driven generator to

Table 4-2 Wind-chill factor

Calm Air	@ 15 MPH	@ 30 MPH	@ 40 MPH
30	9	− 2	− 6
20	− 5	− 18	− 22
10	− 18	− 33	− 38
0	− 31	− 49	− 54
− 10	− 45	− 64	− 70
− 20	− 58	− 78	− 87
− 30	− 72	− 93	−101
− 40	− 85	−109	−116

Note: At − 25 degrees F. skin can freeze in one minute.

Table 4-3 Hypothermic symptoms and treatment

Symptoms
Excessive shivering
Loss of feeling/control of feet and hands
Difficulty in speaking
Drowsiness/exhaustion
Cold extremities

Treatment
Remove person from cause
— out of the cool air temperature
— away from wind
— remove any wet clothing
Warm the victim
— warm bed, heating pad, and the like
— warm the torso first, then the extremities
Seek medical attention if severe

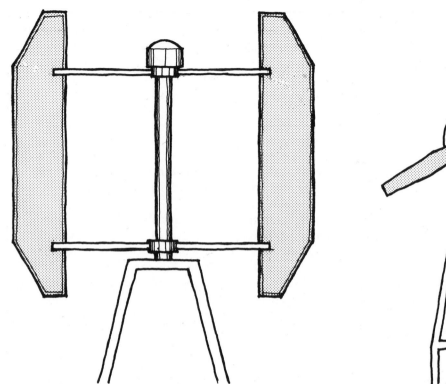

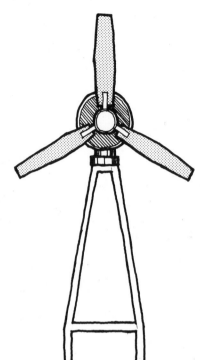

4-15. Wind-driven generators are found in many different sizes and configurations.

work. Some systems will not even turn with winds under that threshold. Most areas of the country do not average 10mph winds over the course of a year and few have sustained winds of 20 to 30 mph, which are the speeds necessary for the generator to work most efficiently. A check with the local weather bureau can tell you if the wind is sufficient in your area.

Obstacles   Although wind speed is important, it is also critical that those winds get to the windmill. If trees, buildings, hills, or other obstacles are between the wind and the windmill, the winds may be blocked, modified, or in some other way made ineffective. Gaining wind-access often requires mounting windmill blades on poles thirty feet tall or higher (fig. 4-16).

Cost   As discussed above, the system's cost versus the cost savings must be carefully analyzed. As with every major purchase, the real cost is not just the initial price of the equipment and installation. Whether the purchase is financed or paid for in cash, there are interest charges or interest lost (in this case interest income from alternative investment) in the expenditure for the system. There are ongoing costs of operation, such as periodic inspections, maintenance, and repair over the lifetime of the system. On the positive side, federal tax credits are available, and your state may also have some type of tax incentive to help defray part of the cost. In addition, as the cost of electricity rises, an existing windmill will pay back its costs that much sooner. However, whether or not to install wind generators is an economic decision and not an emotional one. Talk not only to the wind-generator sales representative but also to your financial planner.

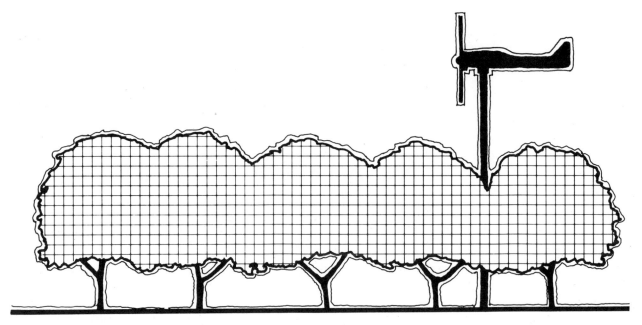

4-16. Windmills are often set above tree level to capture uninterrupted winds.

Zoning/Neighbors   Most books, pamphlets, and magazine articles about windmills show the installed system in a rural location. Since not all of us have the opportunity or desire to live out of the city or suburbs, this example in a rural setting is not practical for most of our needs. Suburban lots, and for that matter most rural lots, are subject to zoning laws and restrictions. These may limit or exclude certain uses, activities, or types of construction on a given piece of ground. Such restrictions may limit the height of a structure or may prohibit any structure, such as a windmill, that is not in character with the surrounding neighborhood. Check with building officials and consult with your neighbors before you take any major steps.

5

Site Selection

SELECTION OF A suitable site for an earth-sheltered home may present some dilemmas. Site suitability is dependent not only upon the physical characteristics of the site and the local zoning ordinances and building codes, but also upon the adaptability of the site to the particular functional relationships of the home envisioned. The search for the optimum south-facing lot with adequate grade change to accommodate a full earth-sheltered home often requires either a smaller community with larger lots or a rural area. Although these locations are best in one sense—they provide abundant space of optimum quality—they present unique problems as well.

Assuming that the basic reasons for choosing an earth-sheltered environment concern energy savings, the move away from urban areas into small towns or rural areas creates energy consumption requirements of a different type. The most obvious is that of increased transportation to and from urban centers. If the optimum site is in a rural area, questions related to conversion of agricultural land and acceptable levels of service also arise.

If the use of the optimum site increases consumption of gasoline, consumes agricultural land, adds to service costs, and increases surrounding land cost, are we in fact conserving or consuming energy (fig. 5-1)?

The following discussion centers around determining site suitability and adaptability *within existing urban/suburban areas.* Not all sites are appropriate for earth-sheltered environments; not all sites are adaptable to earth-sheltered environments. However, if various levels of earth sheltering are considered, most sites can be used. The characteristics of a particular lot can give clues to the amount and type of earth sheltering that is appropriate.

BASIC SITE-SELECTION CONSIDERATIONS

Selection of a site begins with the same general criteria for selecting any home location. However, this section does not discuss location in relation to work, school, commercial, and recreation centers. It assumes that the general location within an urban/suburban area will

84

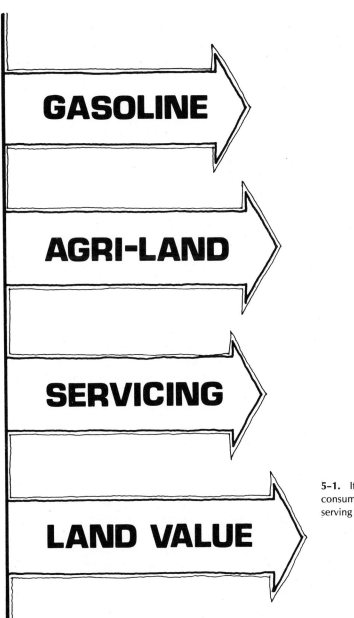

5-1. If using the optimum site increases consumption and adds to cost, are we conserving or consuming energy?

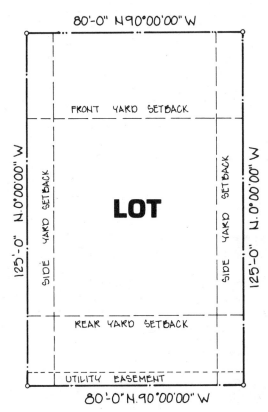

80'-0" N90°00'00" W

FRONT YARD SETBACK

125'-0" N.0°00'00" W

SIDE YARD SETBACK

LOT

SIDE YARD SETBACK

125'-0" N.0°00'00" W

REAR YARD SETBACK

UTILITY EASEMENT

80'-0" N.90°00'00" W

5–2. Each lot has a legally described location and dimensions.

consider the same sort of energy consciousness that leads to earth sheltering.

The following discussion of the basics of site selection assumes the site to be within an urban/suburban area with paved streets and access to public sewers and water supply.

As defined earlier, the land is a composite of soil, slope, and orientation, and it has some type of vegetative cover. Land selected for a site becomes more than a physical entity. The site is a legal and visual entity as well. It has a legally described location and dimensions. The lot is subject to setbacks, easements, zoning ordinances, subdivision regulations, and neighbors' rights (fig. 5–2). The site exists as a visual entity within the neighborhood and has potentially desirable and undesirable on-site and off-site views.

Soils

Soil is the stuff of earth sheltering. It provides the thermal mass that moderates the temperature of the earth-sheltered environment. Important site-selection considerations are the soil's engineering capabilities, subsurface and surface drainage, and its capabilities as a growing medium.

Engineering capabilities of the soil are directly related to the design of the structure. Soil characteristics are important in the design of footings and walls. Some are inappropriate because of the high shrink-swell or high ground water associated with them.

Subsurface drainage, or the lack of it, presents a real limitation to complete earth sheltering. High water tables can cause problems of waterproofing (fig. 5–3).

Surface drainage, determined by a combination of soils, slope, and surrounding conditions, must have a way of exiting the site. Surface-water drainage should either be to the street and into a public storm-collection system or into established waterways leading away from the site. Improper surface drainage can cause waterproofing problems similar to high water-table problems and has the potential of making exterior spaces unusable.

Depth of topsoil, nutrient level, soil moisture, and amount of prior disturbance are all related to the ability of the soil to act as a growing medium. Although it is an important factor in judging the soil, the ability to support growth can be enhanced through site-preparation practices, such as stripping, stockpiling topsoil, construction methods, berms, lightweight soil mixes, and the like.

The most important characteristics, soil-bearing capacity and water-table levels, are the most difficult to get information about inexpensively. Sources of general information include county soil maps, county agricultural-extension offices, and city engineering departments. Local engineering offices and soil-testing companies may be of some assistance as well. People who live adjacent to or within the area of the lot can provide invaluable information based upon observation.

5–3. A high water table can cause problems in waterproofing.

At the site-selection stage, it is important to identify the problems of developing a particular site and to assess the cost of possible mitigation. This effort is critical, but it must be kept in perspective. It is unnecessary to become involved in costly engineering studies at this time. After a particular site or several sites have been located that meet your basic criteria, obtain the necessary further assistance. Engineering expertise related to structure design is essential.

Slope

The slope of the land and the total vertical grade change provide indications of surface drainage and the land's adaptability to earth sheltering. Lot slope must provide for positive surface drainage of water away from the lot to the street or to other drainage systems. Low amounts of slope and small vertical grade changes—flat land—may or may not be a problem. Most sites are adaptable to some level of earth sheltering. Lot size, building envelope, and the area within setbacks and easement lines (fig. 5–4), in combination with slope and grade change, determine the utility of a site for total or partial earth sheltering.

Site Orientation

Site orientation, or the direction of the slope of land, is critical from several perspectives. The ability to capture the warming winter sun and to avoid cold winter winds is enhanced by proper site orientation (fig. 5–5). A site sloping to the south provides opportunities to enhance

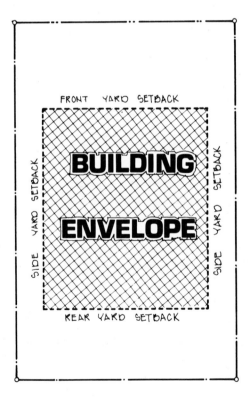

5-4. The building envelope is the area within the yard setbacks and easement lines.

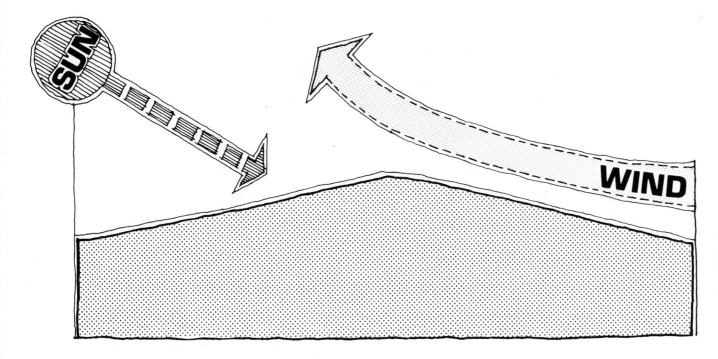

SOUTH FACING   NORTH FACING

5-5. A south-sloping site provides a built-in ability to capture the warming winter sun and to avoid cold winter winds.

solar access and diminish or divert cold winter winds away from the living environment.

Street access is an important consideration of site orientation. Whether street access is on the north or south side plays a major role in determining where building openings will exist for autos and people. In general, lots with street frontage on the north have garages and pedestrian entries to the north, northwest, northeast, east, and west. The impact to energy consumption of these entry orientations can be minimized with sensitive site and structure design, but identifying access orientation is still valuable in measuring the utility of one site over another. If the site can provide proper orientation without manipulation, construction cost will probably be less.

Solar access, or the ability to receive sunlight where it is needed today and in the future, is also an essential consideration (fig. 5-6). The relationship of other structures, evergreen trees, hills, or anything else that will block the low winter sun must be considered. How close is the house or potential solar block to the south line of the lot? Will a "solar window" be available two years from now (fig. 5–7)? Five years from now? Has the community passed an ordinance that ensures solar access? All of these orientation questions need to be addressed.

Vegetation

The vegetation currently existing on a site can be either an asset or a liability. If the lot is in a suburb, the prime vegetation will probably be a mixture of annual and perennial grasses. This type of vegetative cover offers little functional assistance in wind or sun control but at the same time does not impede solar access or cause additional construction costs.

If the site is covered with deciduous trees, care must be taken to determine whether earth sheltering is appropriate or what level of earth sheltering is reasonable. The test of appropriateness and the measure of practicality are easy when there is no tree cover with which to contend. If the site is tree-covered, complete earth sheltering with proper back slopes may begin to jeopardize the existence of the trees by drastically altering (cut or fill) their environment. Sensitive site plan-

5–6. Southern view of a passive-solar earth-sheltered house. Note the newly planted deciduous vegetation that will allow the desired winter sun to reach the house and also will shade the house from the unwanted hot summer sun. Wintertime solar access must be maintained for this structure to function most effectively. (Photograph by Rod Stevens. Courtesy Green Meadows Ltd.)

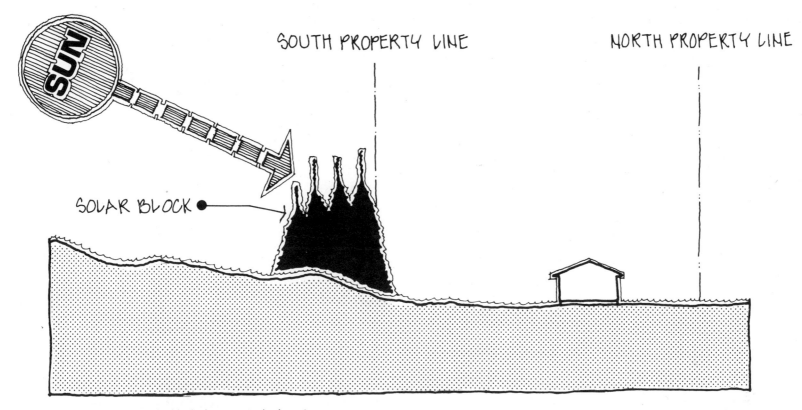

SUN

SOUTH PROPERTY LINE

NORTH PROPERTY LINE

SOLAR BLOCK

5-7. Will solar access be blocked now or in the future?

ning and structure design can ensure that trees on a site do in fact remain an asset and not become a liability.

Zoning and Subdivision Regulations

Review of local regulations, including zoning, that outline the types of uses allowable is essential. In some residential zoning classifications, housing types "not in character" with surrounding neighborhoods may be disallowed. This notion of neighborhood continuity can also arise in the form of deed restrictions or covenants attached to the land.

Front-yard setbacks, utility easements, walkway easements, side-yard setbacks, and rear-yard setbacks are all elements of local subdivision regulations that must be analyzed prior to site selection. Setback requirements can dictate whether an earth-sheltered structure will fit on the site, determine the degree of earth sheltering possible, or can eliminate the possibility of earth sheltering unless a variance to local codes is sought.

Utilities

It is generally assumed that the potential earth-sheltered site is serviced with sewer, water, and public streets, but a word regarding utilities is nonetheless necessary. Sewer elevations in relationship to all floor elevations must be checked. Many homes have been built with basement levels, only to find sewer elevations too shallow to accommodate hookups below the first floor. If it does not eliminate a site, a shallow sewer may greatly alter the degree of earth sheltering possible.

Visual Relationships

Two levels of visual relationships should be considered, the prospect and the aspect.

Prospect (fig. 5–8), the overall view of the neighborhood, is the first level of visual consideration. The neighborhood prospect—that is,

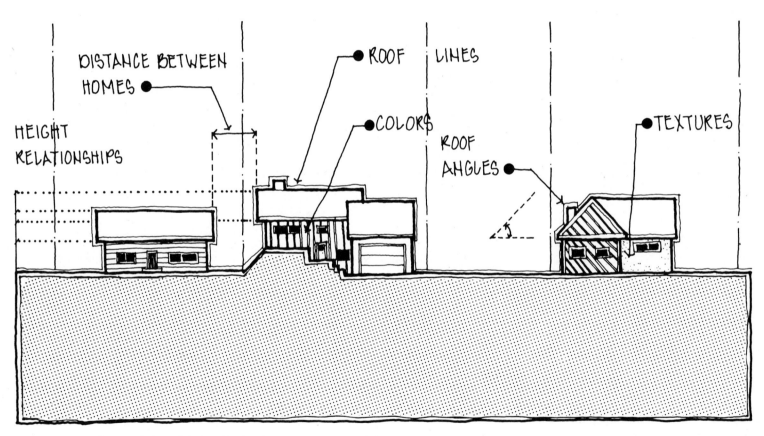

5–8. *Prospect* is the overall view of the neighborhood.

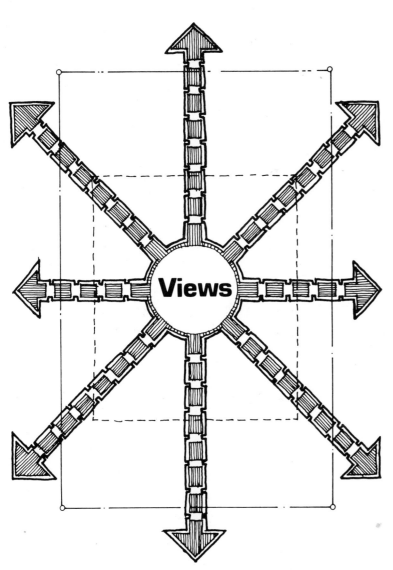

5-9. *Aspect* describes the views from the lot to the surrounding environment.

how new, how traditional, how contemporary, how large, and the visual continuity between and among structures—can indicate whether or not an earth-sheltered environment would be in character and the degree of earth sheltering that would be appropriate.

Aspect (fig. 5-9) is the view from the living areas of the house to the exterior environment and beyond. Are the views from the house desirable? Can less desirable views be screened? Can privacy be created by screening views from without to within?

Purchase Price

A final yet usually neglected selection parameter is the price of the lot itself. South-facing lots with solar access may in the near future begin to bring premium prices on the open market (fig. 5-10). Price of a lot, including financing costs, must be compared to the potential savings expected from developing a more energy-conscious living environment.

GUIDE TO SITE SELECTION

Any site can be planned and designed so that the natural elements (sun, wind, and the like) and the land (slope, orientation, soils, and the like) are recognized and responded to in an energy-conscious and environmentally sound manner.

The following guide provides a relatively simple means of selecting a site for an earth-sheltered environment. It does not replace the involvement of the homeowner, does not excuse the homeowner and/or designer from a complete and thorough knowledge of each candidate site, and it does not supersede common sense. The objective is to bring into focus the suitability of a particular lot for an earth-sheltered environment and/or the degree of earth sheltering appropriate for the lot.

The process outlined is simple. It is a nontechnical method by which the attributes of several lots can be quickly analyzed and assessed. It assumes that the potential owner and/or designer has made a trip to the local county courthouse and has a legal description and a copy of the plat-of-subdivision (legally recorded plan) for each possible lot. With this basic information, the comparison can proceed.

After thorough site investigation regarding soil types and conditions, the analysis and weighting that follows should be completed for each site under investigation. The lots with the highest total points best meet all the necessary parameters.

Soil-bearing Capacity for Footings	Rate
Good bearing capacity	+2
Bearing capacity adequate, can be overcome by minor design modifications	0
Bearing capacity inadequate	−2

Water-table Location	
Water table well below footing level	+2
Water table below footing level, minor waterproofing may be necessary	0
Water table near surface, extensive dewatering necessary	−2

Surface Drainage	
Positive surface-water drainage in two directions from the site	+2
Positive surface-water drainage in one direction from the site	0
No positive surface drainage from the site	−2

Slope/Orientation	
Slope is north to south with adequate vertical change to accommodate full earth shelter	+2
Slope is east-facing	+1
Site is level	0
Slope is west-facing	−1
Slope is north-facing	−2

Vehicular Access	Rate
Vehicular access is from the south	+2
Vehicular access is from the east	+1
Vehicular access is from the west	−1
Vehicular access is from the north	−2

Solar Access	
Solar access guaranteed by local ordinance	+2
Solar access apparent on site; no visible blocks	0
Solar access blocked by evergreen, structure, topography	−2

Vegetation	
Evergreen trees on northern parts of site; deciduous trees on south	+2
Scattered overstory trees that may be used to aid in wind/sun control	0
No vegetation to aid in wind/sun control	−2

Zoning	
Zoning allows earth-sheltered structure—underground	+2
Zoning allows earth-sheltered environment	0
Zoning does not allow earth sheltering—underground	−2

Building Envelope	Rate
Building envelope provides area for east-west orientation of long axis of structure	+2
Building envelope provides area for either southeast-northwest or southwest-northeast orientation of long axis of structure	0
Building envelope provides for north-south orientation of long axis of structure	−2

Utilities	
Sewer elevation adequate to serve lowest floor of structure	+2
Sewer elevation too high to serve lowest floor of structure	−2

Visual Relationships	

Prospect

Earth-sheltered environment compatible with neighborhood character	+2
Modified earth-sheltered environment compatible with neighborhood character	0
Earth-sheltered environment not compatible with neighborhood character	−2

Aspect

Views from the site outward are desirable	+2
Undesirable views can be screened	0
Undesirable views cannot be screened	−2

5-10. Housing sites that allow good solar access may in the near future bring premium prices on the open market. (Photograph by Rod Stevens. Courtesy Green Meadows Ltd.)

ESL	SOILS			WATER TABLE			SURFACE DRAINAGE			SLOPE/ORIENTATION					VEHICULAR ACCESS				SOLAR ACCESS		
	GOOD BEARING CAPACITY	ADEQUATE BEARING CAPACITY	INADEQUATE BEARING CAPACITY	DEEP-BELOW FOOTING LEVEL	BELOW FOOTING LEVEL	SHALLOW-NEAR SURFACE	POSITIVE DRAINAGE-2 DIRECTIONS	POSITIVE DRAINAGE-1 DIRECTION	INADEQUATE DRAINAGE	SOUTH FACING	EAST FACING	LEVEL-NO DIRECTION	WEST FACING	NORTH FACING	SOUTHERN ACCESS	EASTERN ACCESS	WESTERN ACCESS	NORTHERN ACCESS	ACCESS PROTECTED BY ORDINANCE	ACCESS APPARENT ON SITE	ACCESS BLOCKED
RATING	+2	0	-2	+2	-0	-2	+2	0	-2	+2	+1	0	-1	-2	+2	+1	-1	-2	+2	0	-2
LOT A (Address)																					
LOT B (Address)																					
LOT C (Address)			●IF-2 DELETE			●IF-2 DELETE															
LOT D (Address)			◆IF-2			◆IF-2															◆IF-2 DELETE-ALTER?

5-11. Lot comparison chart.

VEGETATION			ZONING			BUILDING ENVELOPE				SEWER		VISUAL RELATIONSHIPS							
												PROSPECT			ASPECT				
EVERGREEN-NORTH; DECIDUOUS-SOUTH	SCATTERED OVERSTORY	NO VEGETATION	ALLOWS UNDERGROUND	ALLOWS EARTH SHELTERING	UNDERGROUND NOT ALLOWED	EAST-WEST ENVELOPE	SOUTHEAST-NORTHWEST ENVELOPE	SOUTHWEST-NORTHEAST ENVELOPE	NORTH-SOUTH ENVELOPE	SEWER DEPTH ADEQUATE	SEWER DEPTH INADEQUATE	COMPATIBLE WITH NEIGHBORHOOD	COMPATIBLE IF MODIFIED	INCOMPATIBLE WITH NEIGHBORHOOD	DESIRABLE VIEWS	UNDESIRABLE VIEWS SCREENABLE	UNDESIRABLE VIEWS NOT SCREENABLE	TOTAL	RANK
+2	0	-2	+2	0	-2	+2	0	0	-2	+2	-2	+2	0	-2	+2	0	-2		
					◆ IF-2 DELETE-ALTER-VARIANCE						◆ IF-2 DELETE-ALTER-PUMP								

If either the bearing capacity or the water table show up as −2, serious thought should be given to eliminating the site from consideration. If, however, the site has other attributes that make it preferable, now is the time to get professional advice regarding the expense of overcoming inappropriate soil or high water tables.

This evaluation procedure can provide assistance in deciding which of the candidate lots is most suitable. It may well provide an easy method of deciding which single lot is the most appropriate. What will probably happen, however, is that several lots will have similar scores and a second look will be necessary. They can then be compared by individual category scores. Such comparison—by soil, for example—may help create some notions of the steps that must be taken to mitigate less than desired site conditions.

At this point, the cost of the lot may be related to the amount of site manipulation or structure manipulation necessary to overcome deficiencies. The cost should be factored in after summarizing the guideline analysis.

Lot-cost comparison can provide an additional level of comparison.

By comparing raw lot costs with how well each lot meets desired conditions and how much must be done in terms of alteration or design changes, a more realistic cost can be developed.

Summary

A. mentioned earlier, this comparison procedure is meant to aid in selection of a site for an earth-sheltered environment. The procedure itself causes the owner and/or designer to become more aware of physical, legal, and visual realities. It does not attempt to replace individual decision making, only to aid in the application of common sense.

Figure 5–11 is set up to allow for the comparison of selected lots. By looking at each lot individually and rating it based upon the scale provided, a simple, more complete comparison of the overall suitability of one lot to another can be achieved. Problem areas of individual lots can be evaluated to determine the extent of each. Following through with this evaluation process can expand knowledge of and sensitivity to each of the parameters.

Site Planning

AFTER SELECTING a site with southern exposure that is appropriate or adaptable to an earth-sheltered environment, design of the particular earth-sheltered environment, unit, and site can continue. Stock plans (general plans that can be adapted to any situation) are available at a reasonable price in many local bookstores. Particular site characteristics, neighborhood character, family requirements, price range, and other criteria determine final house plans. If stock plans meet all the requirements, the plans are appropriate. If they do not, which is usually the case, several alternatives exist.

The first line of adjustment usually starts by altering the site to meet the requirement of the plan. This is the conventional mode of operation, the accepted norm of site sensitivity. The alternative involves adjusting the house plan to meet all the criteria, not only those easiest to deal with. A new home should meet the needs of the new homeowners in the way they envision.

To better understand and identify what needs to be adjusted to create the house/lot fit, a more complete look at the lot is necessary.

PLANNING PROCESS

The site-selection process identified basic site opportunities and constraints that established the criteria for site planning. The site-planning process for an earth-sheltered environment is similar to the process used for most site plans. This process includes site inventory, site analysis, program development, and unit and site design (fig. 6-1). The phases, site inventory through site design, are sequential—that is, the information gained from one phase establishes the basis for the next. This type of building-block progression is simple in theory and logical in practice. Although the process is shown as sequential, references will be made to prior steps, information, and ideas to help guide decisions.

SITE INVENTORY

Site inventory identifies the elements necessary for decision making. The information acquired in the site-selection process provides a basis for this phase. All the physical factors (soils, slopes, vegetation, subsurface and surface water) should be documented.

The surest way to gain complete and accurate base information is to have a professional land surveyor or engineer prepare a survey. This survey (fig. 6-2) should include property boundaries, corners, setbacks (front, side, and rear yard), utility easements, utility locations, walkway easements, location and elevation of any trees or other special elements on the lot, and topography.

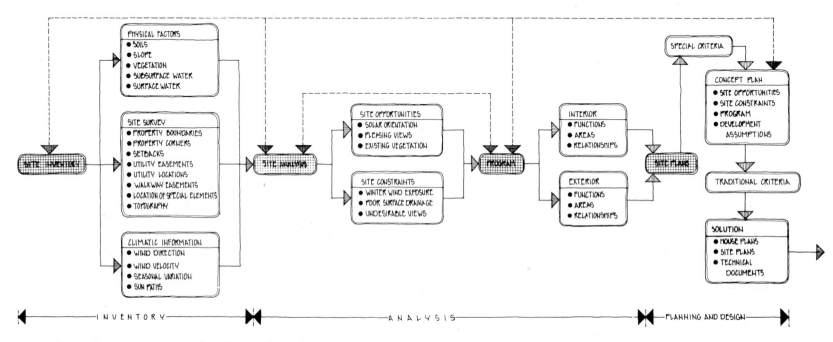

6–1. The site-planning process is simple in theory and logical in practice.

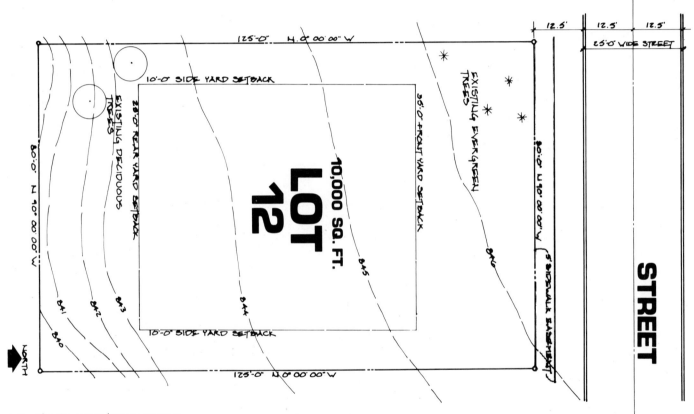

6-2. The site survey locates property boundaries, property corners, setbacks, and easements.

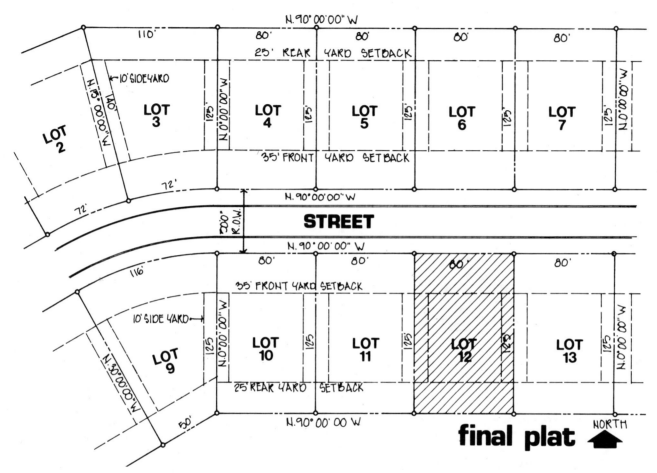

6–3. Plats may be available for some of the base information.

In many newer subdivisions, a plat of individual lots is available (fig. 6–3). It can provide boundary, setback, and other legal information. The land surveyor or engineer should review the plat, locate the property corners on the site, and prepare a topographic map that shows site elevations.

In addition to the physical factors, boundary survey, and topography, climatic information—sun paths and wind direction and velocity through the seasons of the year—should be indicated. Again, this information is available from the nearest weather-bureau office.

SITE ANALYSIS

The site analysis (fig. 6–4) establishes site characteristics and design criteria. *Site opportunities,* such as solar orientation, pleasing views, and existing vegetation, are documented. These existing elements can be used with little modification. *Site constraints,* such as exposure to winter winds, drainage problems, and poor views, are indications that some action must take place to overcome the constraint. The location of the house itself should take advantage of opportunities (good views and solar exposure), while at the same time responding to constraints (winter winds and poor views). Response to both opportunities and constraints is dependent upon what you want to occur on the site.

PROGRAM

The program includes the structure and the site. Quite often structures are programmed without considering site implications, exterior uses, or the transition between exterior and interior uses. Since the program is a documentation of basic needs and desires, the users—whether a family, a couple, a group, or an individual—should be involved in its development. This is true whether a professional designer is used or not. The program identifies functions, areas, and relationships for interior, exterior, and transition spaces. A simple way to help develop the program is to write a list of all the functions desired that re-

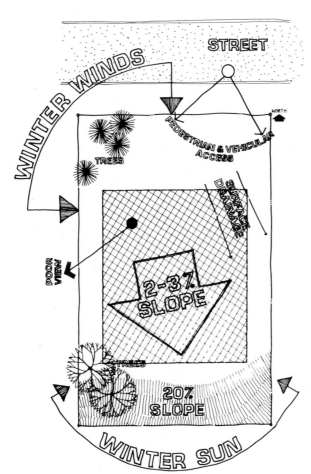

6-4. The site analysis indicates the character of the site in a more specific manner.

Program Sheet*

☐ INTERIOR   ☐ EXTERIOR   ☐ TRANSITION

FUNCTION:_____

_____

CONSTRUCTION IMPLICATIONS:
MECHANICAL:_____

_____

AREA REQUIREMENTS:_____

_____

_____

_____

ELECTRICAL:_____

_____

_____

RELATIONSHIPS TO OTHER FUNCTIONS:
DIRECT:_____

_____

_____

OTHER COMMENTS:_____

_____

_____

INDIRECT:_____

_____

_____

_____

_____

_____

*EACH FUNCTION WILL HAVE A PROGRAM SHEET

6–5. What is desired, its size, and the relationship among the functions constitute a basic program.

quire space within the house (such as living, dining, cooking, sleeping, laundry, storage), and all of the functions desired that require space in the exterior environment (eating, sunning, relaxing, swimming, children's play areas, adult congregation areas, garden, parking, and so on). Each member of the user group should develop the list independently. Questions related to how large areas ought to be can be answered by personal preference, by building codes, and/or by budget limitations. Then, after discussion, the lists are combined to form a clear representation of the group's collective desires.

If you know which functions you want and how large an area each will require, the last element of the program is to determine how the functions should relate to one another. Is the kitchen near the dining room or open to it? Does the family room open onto the deck? Is the children's play area visible from the deck? Each function identified will have a set of desired relationships. These three elements—what is desired, how much or how large, and the relationship among functions—constitute a basic program (fig. 6–5). How these functions are placed upon the site depends on the site opportunities and constraints.

CONCEPT DEVELOPMENT

Simply stated, concept development (fig. 6–6) is the combination of site opportunities and constraints with the program. This is usually the most difficult phase. If some of the program or site constraints are neglected, the process is much easier—but do not do it! The more problems resolved at this stage, the better the solution and thus the final living environment.

The concept shows the assumptions pertaining to general development, such as mitigating the winter winds (fig. 6–7) and taking advantage of the winter sun (fig. 6–8), as well as responses to individual opportunities and/or constraints.

The screening of undesirable off-site views, access to parking, general location of interior and exterior activities, and the relationship among the activities and the site are demonstrated on the concept plan.

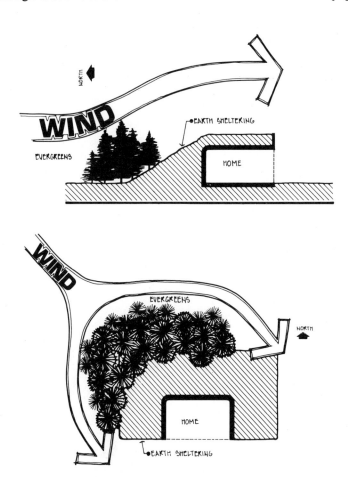

6–6. The concept is the combination of site opportunities and constraints with the program.

6–7. The concept establishes the assumptions of general development, such as mitigating the winter winds.

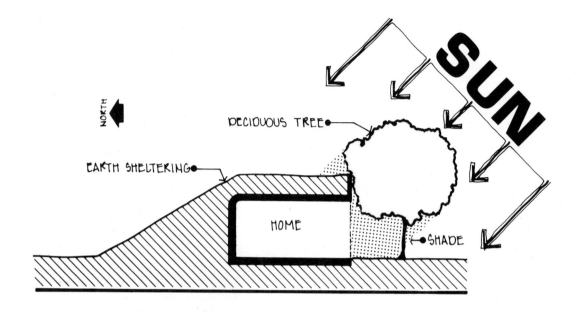

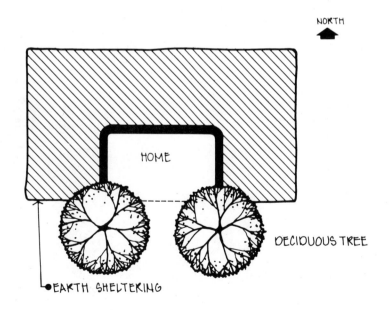

6-8. Sun control in mitigating summer sun while assuring winter solar access is an underlying assumption of concept development.

THE SOLUTION

The solution is in the form of house plans, technical documents that guide construction of the structure, and a site plan that guides how and where the structure is placed, how and where exterior uses will occur, and how and where transition spaces occur. These final plans can and will occur in many forms. They can be very sophisticated, prepared by architects, landscape architects, and designers, or they can be very basic, such as those used by a homeowner working with a builder. Regardless of who prepares the plans, the solution must be user- and environment-responsive.

Special Criteria

A special set of criteria must be considered when preparing a final plan for earth-sheltered landscapes. The location of street access—whether predominantly north or south—are two general delineations that begin to establish site criteria. Both assume proper distribution—that is, buffer spaces to the north and living spaces to the south.

Many derivations can be drawn from these two delineations. However, the differing factor is whether the north exposure remains totally sheltered by earth or is broken to provide access to vehicles or people (fig. 6–9).

Case One, street access from the north (fig. 6–10), provides both

6–9. Earth-sheltering may be interrupted to provide access for vehicles or people. (Photograph by Rod Stevens. Courtesy Green Meadows Ltd.)

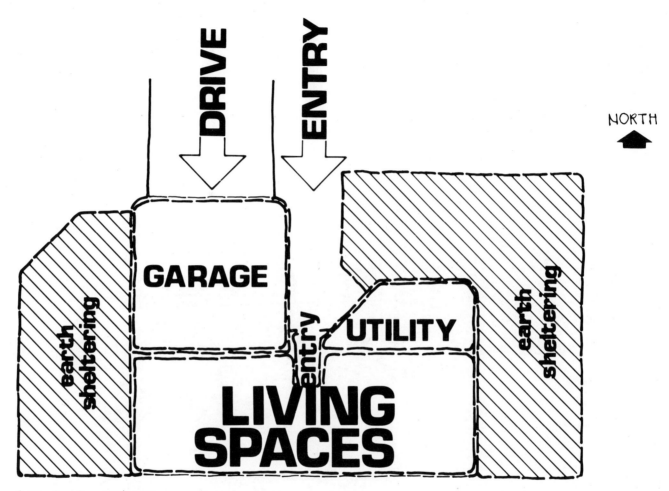

6-10. Case One. North entry.

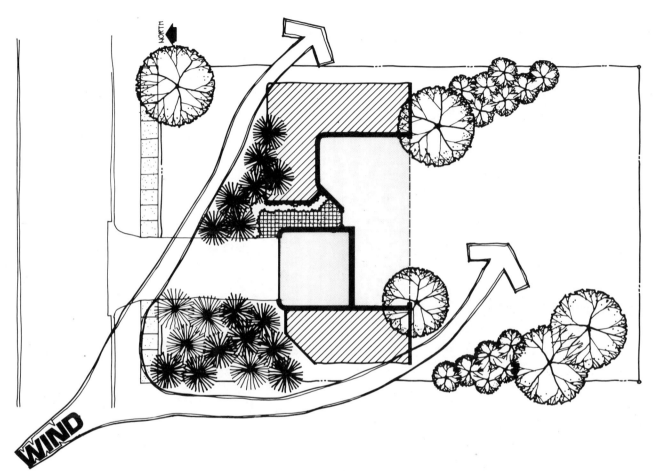

6-11. When vehicular or pedestrian access is from the north, winter winds should be channeled away from openings.

auto and pedestrian access on the side of the house that suffers the most severe winter exposure and offers the basis for earth sheltering—protection from cold winter winds. This case gives special attention to how winter winds are directed and controlled. In addition to evergreen plantings, earth berming can direct the winter winds away from garage doors and front doors (fig. 6–11). Placement of the front door so that the mass of the garage directs wind away from it will,

when combined with plantings and berms, greatly reduce the effect of the cold winds (fig. 6–12).

Case Two, street access from the south (fig. 6–13), provides a more proper relationship technically—that is, no openings to the north. This case does, however, introduce pedestrians and passersby into the living spaces. Remember, proper passive-solar utilization puts buffer spaces on the north and living spaces on the south. This case gives special at-

6–12. Sheltering the main entrance to the structure, such as the pedestrian entrance on this house, can reduce the impact of winds upon the interior. (Photograph by Rod Stevens. Courtesy Green Meadows Ltd.)

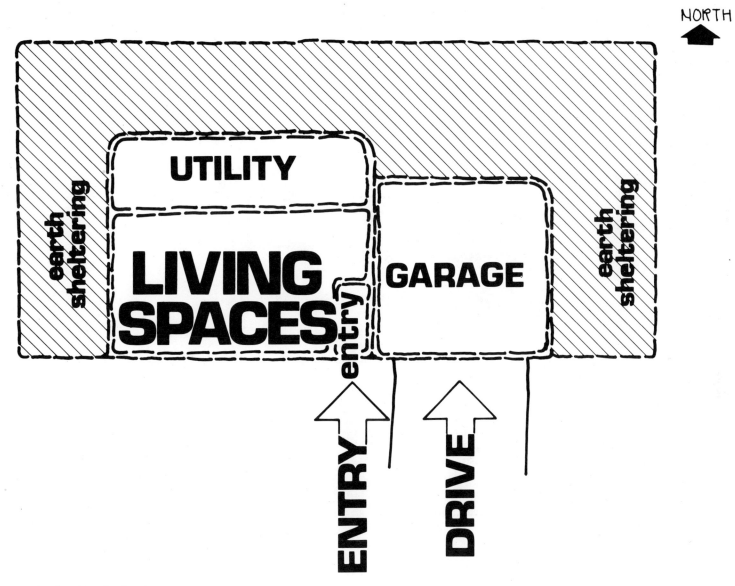

6-13. Case Two. South entry.

tention to visual relationships created by the functional requirements, particularly the sense of entry/arrival and privacy (fig. 6–14).

Common to both cases is the criterion that cold winter winds be mitigated, warming winter sun be used, cooling summer breezes be maximized, and hot summer sun be minimized.

Conventional housing styles that depend upon mechanical heating and cooling systems for comfort ignore the basic environmental criteria. In other words, windows and openings are located without re-

gard to cold winds or warming sun. Visual contact from interior to exterior is often four-directional (fig. 6–15).

The difference in visual contact from the interior to the exterior between conventional housing and earth-sheltered structures establishes additional special criteria. Probably one of the most neglected areas in the design and site planning of earth-sheltered environments is in recognizing and coping with the change in visual relationships. These changes are of two basic types. They are described by the same terms

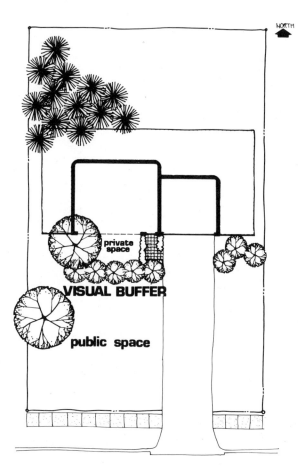

6–14. When vehicular and pedestrian access is from the south, visual buffers between public exterior spaces and private interior spaces should be considered.

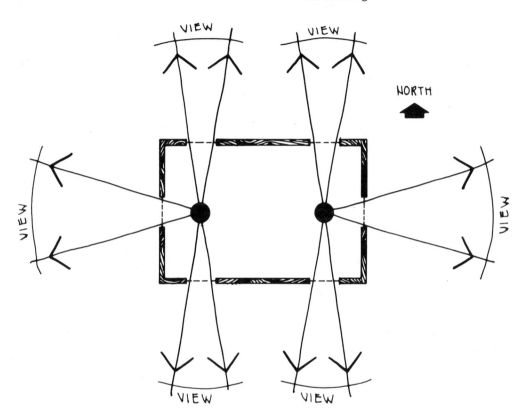

6–15. Most conventional homes have windows on all sides.

used earlier in the criteria for site selection. First, *prospect,* outside the environment looking in; second, *aspect,* inside looking out.

Prospect   Prospect, which is the overall view of the neighborhood, must be recognized when design begins. Design of an earth-sheltered home within an area of conventional one- and two-story homes should respond to the overall visual character already established. Identifying neighborhood character and applying that to the two cases mentioned can help in determining the level of earth sheltering appropriate for a neighborhood.

Case One, with vehicle access on the north, assumes that an above-grade garage directly associated with the street will be provided. In a condition where full earth sheltering is possible, the garage itself becomes the element of adaptation to neighborhood character. How the garage is designed, relationships to entry spaces, and relationships to surrounding structures will determine neighborhood fit. Many varying definitions of neighborhood character have been and will continue to be formed. In some neighborhoods, an identifiable architectural style is very apparent. Take cues from whatever the style is and use facade, trim, color, and massing to harmonize rather than contrast with what exists. More likely than a single architectural style is a combination of many styles, many variations on a few themes. Important cues in these neighborhoods are the scale (one-story, two-story, and so on), the massing, closeness of units to one another, closeness of units to streets, and color ranges.

Case Two, with vehicular access from the south, provides the opportunity for a more traditional garage/entry relationship. This relationship makes fitting into a variety of neighborhoods an easier task.

Creating visual harmony within a neighborhood does not mean strict repetition or duplication of what exists; it means maintaining the essence of the neighborhood character by continuing visible elements of the neighborhood—adding threads to the urban fabric.

Aspect   Aspect, which is the visual relationship from within the unit to the exterior environment, has been altered by responding to the basic criteria. By turning our backs to cold winter winds, we also remove visual contact in that direction—few, if any, windows on the north, west, and east. The amount of change in aspect depends not only on the particular case, but also on the degree of earth sheltering used.

In Case One, the visual field is either a dual or a multiple field. Multiple-field aspect (fig. 6-16) describes visual relationships that occur when visual access to the exterior is provided simultaneously by the southern exposure and by the vehicular and pedestrian access on

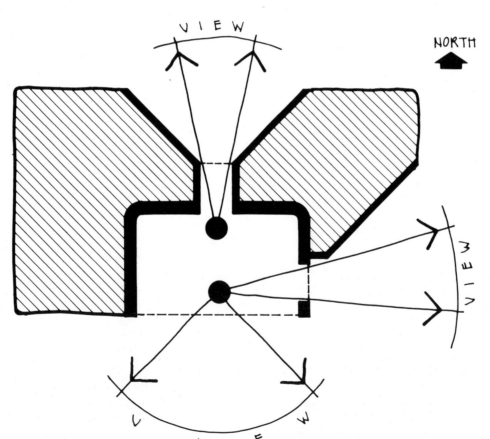

6-16. Multiple field. Visual field is limited to three directions (Case One).

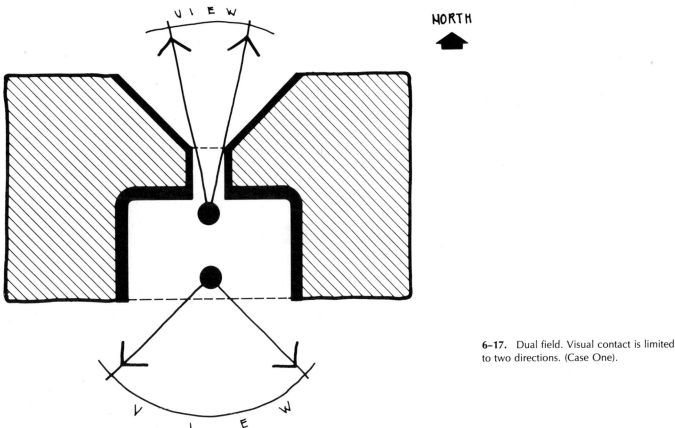

6-17. Dual field. Visual contact is limited to two directions. (Case One).

the north. Visual access to three or more sides provides three-directional visual contact.

Dual-field aspect describes visual relationships that can occur in both cases. Simply stated, it is visual contact in two directions, either north and south in Case One (fig. 6-17) or south and east in Case Two (fig. 6-18).

In addition to the dual field, Case Two can also have single-field or one-directional (southern) visual contact (fig. 6-19).

The visual relationships, prospect and aspect, are important in developing a sense of fit within a neighborhood and understanding and maximizing visual relationships from within the earth-sheltered environment.

Traditional Criteria

In addition to the special conditions created by earth-sheltered environments, traditional elements of design come into play when moving from a conceptual plan to a definitive final plan. The following is a brief discussion of these elements.

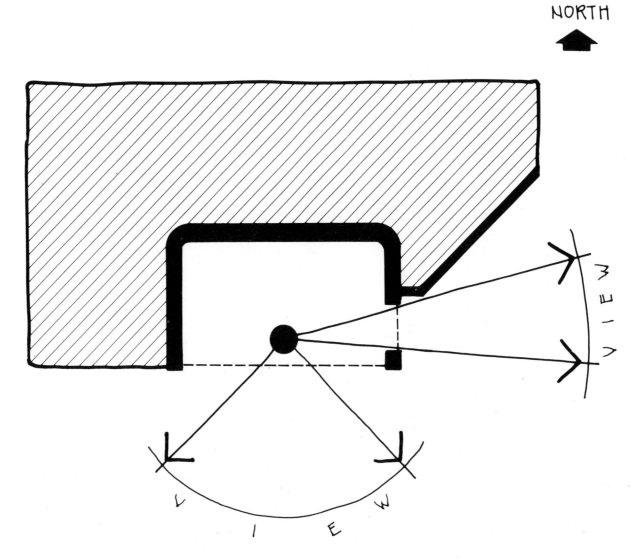

6-18. Dual field. Visual contact is limited to two directions. (Case Two).

NORTH

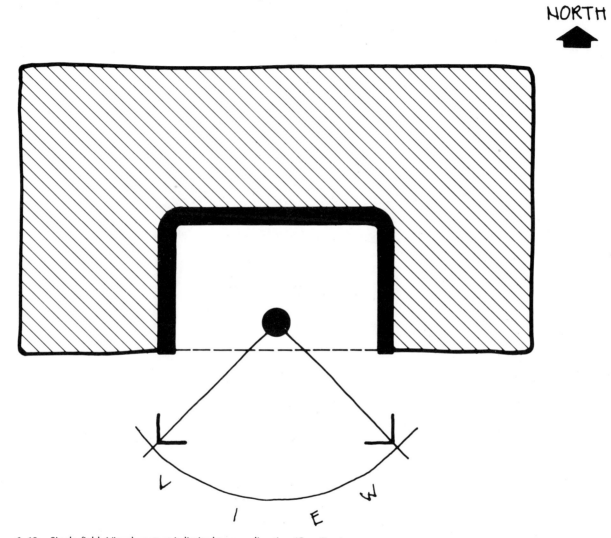

6-19. Single field. Visual contact is limited to one direction (Case Two).

Color   The use of color can make distant views seem closer or close views seem further away. Emotional responses, such as of solitude or excitement, can be enhanced by the use of color. Color can also provide emphasis in a space. Bright, exciting colors can and should be used to give seasonal and periodic interest to the landscape.

Form   Form in the earth-sheltered landscape is created by architectural elements (such as walls, trellis, and fences), plant material (such as trees and shrubs), the earth in the form of earth berms, and all of these in combination. The form of an exterior space can make that space foreboding or inviting, intimate or grandiose. In combination with other design elements, form can create a comfortable environment.

Texture   Texture is the visual and tactile quality of the surface. Recognizing and using it as a design element, in combination with other design elements, can directly expand or contract the perception of space. Texture can be used in the form of plant material, paving, and the like, to create transitions by moving from fine to medium to coarse textures. By putting coarse textures in the foreground, then making a transition from coarse to medium to fine texture in the background, a space can be given greater visual depth. Such a use of texture can make small spaces seem larger or large spaces seem more intimate.

Proportion, balance, sequence, and the illusion of space are all achieved with the use of color, form, and texture in relation to physical characteristics such as fences, trellises, pools, walks, decks, trees, shrubs, and ground cover.

The selection of paving textures or plants that achieve the emotional or visual responses you desire is a task that requires a great deal of time and thought. How well the concept is transformed into a final plan and then into a living environment will depend on many factors. Aside from using professional designers, the other major factor in ensuring the creation of an environment that successfully achieves the objectives of the owner is the extent to which the process—site inventory, site analysis, program development, concept development, and solution—is applied.

Bibliography

American Society of Landscape Architects Foundation. *Landscape Planning for Energy Conservation*. Reston, Virginia: Environmental Design Press, 1979.

Anderson, Bruce, and Well, Malcolm. *Passive Solar Energy—The Homeowner's Guide to Natural Heating and Cooling*. Andover, Massachusetts: Brick House Publishing Company, 1981.

"Bulletin." *Stereo Review,* January 1983, p. 5.

Campbell, Stu. *The Underground House Book*. Charlotte, Vermont: A Garden Way Book, 1980.

Civil Engineering—ASCE (Magazine). May 1980.

"Climatic Changes Produced by Cities." Mimeographed. Department of Landscape Architecture, University of Wisconsin, Madison, Wisconsin, 1974.

Committee on Remote Sensing for Agricultural Purposes. *Remote Sensing with Special Reference to Agriculture and Forestry*. Washington, D.C.: National Academy of Sciences, 1970.

Core, Earl J. *Plant Taxonomy*. Englewood Cliffs, New Jersey: Prentice-Hall, Inc., 1955.

Corn . . . Alcohol . . . Farm Fuel! Iowa Corn Promotion Board and Iowa Development Commission, n.d.

Curtis, John T. *The Vegetation of Wisconsin*. Madison, Wisconsin: The University of Wisconsin Press, 1959.

DeBord, David D. "The Restoration of Prairies and Other Native Plant Communities as a Landscape Design Alternative." Master's Thesis, University of Wisconsin, 1975.

Dick, Everett. *The Sod-House Frontier 1854-1890*. Lincoln, Nebraska: Johnsen Publishing Company.

Energy Efficient Buildings: An Architectural Record Book. New York: McGraw-Hill Book Company, 1980.

Energy from the Winds. United States Department of Energy. DOE/PA-0013 (2-80). Washington, D.C.: U.S. Government Printing Office.

"Energy-Saving Concepts Applicable to Landscapes." *Weeds, Trees and Turf,* February 1980, pp. 17-21, 92.

Fact Sheet: Energy Conservation in the Rural Home. United States Department of Agriculture. AFS-2-3-8. Washington, D.C.: U.S. Government Printing Office, 1980.

Fact Sheet: Energy Conservation in the Rural Home. United States Department of Agriculture. AFS-2-3-15, 1981. Washington, D.C.: U.S. Government Printing Office, 1981.

Fourth Annual Iowa Solar Operational Results Conference Proceedings. Des Moines, Iowa: 1980.

Frenette, Edward R. *Earth Sheltering: The Form of Energy and the Energy of Form*. New York: Pergamon Press, 1981.

Geothermal Energy. United States Department of Energy, Office of Public Affairs. DOE/OPA-0051 (11-79). Washington, D.C.: U.S. Government Printing Office, 1980.

Heating with Wood. United States Department of Energy. DOE/CS-0158, 1980.

Heiting, W. Tony. *Solar Energy—An Iowa Energy Policy Council Update.* Des Moines, Iowa: Iowa Energy Policy Council, 1978.

Hodges, Laurent. *Solar Radiation in Iowa.* Ames, Iowa: Iowa Energy Extension Service. EES-48, 1982.

Hodges, Laurent. *Super-Insulation for Iowa.* Ames, Iowa: Iowa Energy Extension Service. EES-46, 1982.

Housing at the Turning Point. National Association of Home Builders. Official Report, 1981.

How to Understand Your Utility Bill. United States Department of Energy. DOE/PA-0010 (Rev. 2-80). Washington, D.C.: U.S. Government Printing Office.

Huelman, Pat, and Barron-Penfold, Teddi. *Solar Retrofit: What are the Options?* Ames, Iowa: Iowa Energy Extension Service. EES-39, 1982.

Jaffe, Martin, and Erley, Duncan. *Protecting Solar Access for Residential Development—A Guidebook for Planning Officials.* Chicago, Illinois: The American Planning Association, 1979.

Jaffe, Martin, and Erley, Duncan. *Residential Solar Design Review—A Manual on Community Architectural Controls and Solar Energy Use.* Chicago, Illinois: The American Planning Association, 1980.

Kroner, Walter, and Haviland, David. *Passive Design Ideas for the Energy Conscious Architect.* Rockville, Maryland: National Solar Heating and Cooling Information Center, 1978.

Mazria, Edward. *The Passive Solar Energy Book.* Emmaus, Pennsylvania: Rodale Press, 1979.

METRIA: 3. Proceedings of the Third Conference of the Metropolitan Tree Improvement Alliance. Rutgers—The State University of New Jersey: 1980.

Morrison, James. W. *The Complete Energy-Saving Handbook for Homeowners.* New York: Harper and Row Publishers, 1980.

Mudrak, Louise; Lassoie, James; McGaw, Cynthia; and Himel, James. *Urban Vegetation: A Reference for New York Communities.* United States Department of Agriculture. Ithaca, New York: Department of Natural Resources, Cornell University.

"Natural Gas Price Up, Up—Way High Up." *Des Moines Tribune,* 12 February 1982.

"OPEC Cuts Price of Oil by $5 to $29 a Barrel." *Des Moines Register,* 15 March 1983.

Passive Design: It's a Natural. Golden, Colorado: SERI, A Division of Midwest Research Institute, 1980.

Passive Design Ideas for the Energy-Conscious Builder. Rockville, Maryland: United States Department of Energy, A National Solar Heating and Cooling Center Publication. August 1978.

Passive Solar Design Handbook, Vol. I: Passive Solar Design Concepts. Prepared by Total Environment Action, Inc. for United States Department of Energy, 1980. Washington, D.C.: U.S. Government Printing Office, 1980.

Passive Solar Information Manual. Des Moines, Iowa: Iowa Energy Policy Council, 1981.

Powell, Jeanne W. *An Economic Model for Passive Solar Designs in Commercial Environments.* NBS Building Series 125: *Solar Cities.* United States Department of Commerce, 1980. Washington, D.C.: U.S. Government Printing Office, 1980.

Proceedings of the Midwest Earth Shelter Conference. Omaha, Nebraska: 1981.

Proceedings of the National Urban Forestry Conference, Vols. I and II. Washington, D.C.: College of Environmental Science and Forestry, State University of New York, and United States Department of Agriculture Forest Service. Syracuse, New York: 1978.

Ramsey, Charles George, and Sleeper, Harold Reeve. *Architectural Graphic Standards,* Fifth Ed. New York: John Wiley and Sons, Inc., 1961.

Rideout, Edward H., and Isacson, Orjan E. *Energy Systems 1980-81.* Woburn, Massachusetts: Technical Handbook Publications, 1980.

Second Annual Iowa Solar Operational Results Conference Proceedings. Des Moines, Iowa: 1980.

Soil Survey Maps, Polk County, Iowa. Series 1953, No. 9. United States Department of Agriculture, 1959. Washington, D.C.: U.S. Government Printing Office.

Solar Energy. United States Department of Energy. DOE/PA-0016 (12-79). Washington, D.C.: U.S. Government Printing Office.

Southwick, Charles H. *Ecology and the Quality of our Environment.* New York: Van Nostrand Reinhold Company, 1972.

Third Annual Iowa Solar Operational Results Conference Proceedings. Des Moines, Iowa: 1982.

Thomas, William. "Notes of a Disappointed China Traveler." *Planning,* February 1982, pp. 17-19.

Tips for Energy Savers. United States Department of Energy. DOE/OPA-0037, 1978. Washington, D.C.: U.S. Government Printing Office: 1979.

Underground Homes: Information Manual. Compilation of Information from *Underground Homes.* Portsmouth, Ohio.

Underground Space Center, University of Minnesota. *Earth Sheltered Homes: Plans and Designs.* New York: Van Nostrand Reinhold Company, 1981.

Underground Space Center, University of Minnesota. *Earth Sheltered Housing Design: Guidelines, Examples, and References.* New York: Van Nostrand Reinhold Company, 1979.

Underground Space Center, University of Minnesota. *Earth Sheltered Residential Design Manual.* New York: Van Nostrand Reinhold Company, 1982.

United States Department of Energy. *Proceedings of the Annual DOE Active Solar Heating and Cooling Contractors' Review Meeting.* Incline Village, Nevada: 1980.

Watts, May Theilgaard. *Reading the Landscape of America.* New York: Macmillan Publishing Co., Inc, 1975.

Winter Survival: A Consumer's Guide to Winter Preparedness. United States Department of Energy. DOE/OPA-0019R (9-80). Washington, D.C.: U.S. Government Printing Office: 1980.

Wright, Sidney and Rodney; Selby, Bob; and Dieckmann, Larry. *The Hawkweed Passive Solar House Book.* Chicago: Rand McNally and Company, 1980.

Zachary, A. L., and Franzmeier, D. P. "Handbook for Region III Soils Contest." Mimeographed. 1972.

Index